Web Design

Prentice Hall
is an imprint of

Harlow, England • London • New York • Boston • San Francisco • Toronto • Sydney • Singapore • Hong Kong
Tokyo • Seoul • Taipei • New Delhi • Cape Town • Madrid • Mexico City • Amsterdam • Munich • Paris • Milan

PEARSON EDUCATION LIMITED

Edinburgh Gate
Harlow CM20 2JE
Tel: +44 (0)1279 623623
Fax: +44 (0)1279 431059
Website: www.pearsoned.co.uk

First published in Great Britain in 2010

© James A. Brannan 2010

The right of James A. Brannan to be identified as author of this work has been asserted
by him in accordance with the Copyright, Designs and Patents Act 1988.

ISBN: 978-0-273-72353-0

British Library Cataloguing-in-Publication Data
A catalogue record for this book is available from the British Library

Library of Congress Cataloging-in-Publication Data
Brannan, James A.
 Web design in simple steps / James A. Brannan
      p. cm.
 ISBN 978-0-273-72353-0 (pbk.)
 1. Web sites--Design. I. Title.
 TK5105.888B7246 2010
 006.7--dc22
                        2009038633

10 9 8 7 6 5 4 3 2 1
13 12 11 10 09

Designed by pentacorbig, High Wycombe
Typeset in 11/14 pt ITC Stone Sans by 30
Printed and bound Rotollto Lombarda, Italy

The publisher's policy is to use paper manufactured from sustainable forests.

Web Design

in Simple steps

James A. Brannan

Use your computer with confidence

Get to grips with practical computing tasks with minimal time, fuss and bother.

In Simple Steps guides guarantee immediate results. They tell you everything you need to know on a specific application; from the most essential tasks to master, to every activity you'll want to accomplish, through to solving the most common problems you'll encounter.

Helpful features

To build your confidence and help you to get the most out of your computer, practical hints, tips and shortcuts feature on every page:

ALERT: Explains and provides practical solutions to the most commonly encountered problems

HOT TIP: Time and effort saving shortcuts

SEE ALSO: Points you to other related tasks and information

DID YOU KNOW? Additional features to explore

WHAT DOES THIS MEAN?
Jargon and technical terms explained in plain English

Practical. Simple. Fast.

in Simple steps

Dedication:

For Lee Borup and Weber State University's Veterans Upward Bound (VUB) Project. A chance encounter opened an entirely new world. Had we never met, I would never have acquired an education or written this book.

Author acknowledgments:

Thanks to the staff at Pearson, especially Katy Robinson, Steve Temblett and Emma Devlin. Also thanks to Neil Salkind. Thanks to the many sites that graciously allowed me to use screenshots from their sites. Special thanks to Everaldo and his open source Crystal Project icons, www.everaldo.com, these icons are beautiful and make my books much nicer.

in Simple steps

Contents at a glance

Top 10 Web Design
Problems Solved

Contents

2 Website architecture

3 Writing your text

10 Testing your website

Top 10 Web Design Problems Solved

Top 10 Web Design Tips

Tip 1: Remember, the entire world is your audience

Why begin a web design book with this as its number one tip? Just take a look at this tip's webpage, that's why – and no, it's not me. Remember, the entire world is your audience. When developing personal websites, it is all too easy to forget the Internet is a portal to the world. It feels so personal and private in the confines of your study: it is not.

1. Chatting on webcam sites, Stickam for instance, is all the rage with teens and students these days. Being naïve, they think it is semi-private: it is not. Nothing is private on the Internet.

2. Look up 'blogging and fired from work' and you will find many links to people who have been fired for the content of their blogs. A blog is not private, it is public: remember that. Do not use a blog for therapy unless you really want to air all your dirty laundry and are willing to face the consequences.

3. Remember, your sites can and will influence others. A site can invoke violence. You might think something is just a joke, but Scotland Yard might not think so. Websites, despite their ease of creation, are a very public medium.

? DID YOU KNOW?

The donkey is from Flickr.com and was taken by Kevin Law, and is released under the Creative Commons Attribution licence.

WHAT DOES THIS MEAN?

Stickam: a social networking site where users can broadcast using a webcam.

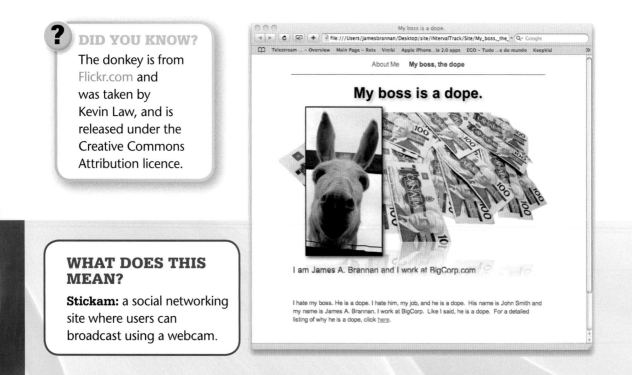

Tip 2: Provide a service

This tip should arguably be the number one tip. As you will see, throughout this book I repeat the mantra 'users come to your site to fulfil a need, not to bask in your design brilliance'. You fulfil needs by providing a service. If you remember nothing else from this book, remember this tip.

1 This book's entire premise is related to this tip, particularly Chapter 1. When finished with this book, review the websites mentioned throughout and think about the services each one provides.

2 Follow the steps presented in Chapter 1 to try to determine the services your site might provide – before you start analysis and design!

3 If interested in learning more, navigate to Wikipedia and look up Web 2.0. Web 2.0 design is strongly focused on offering services to users.

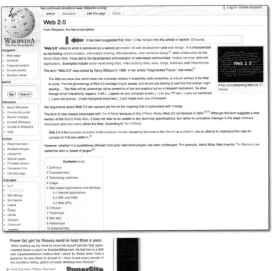

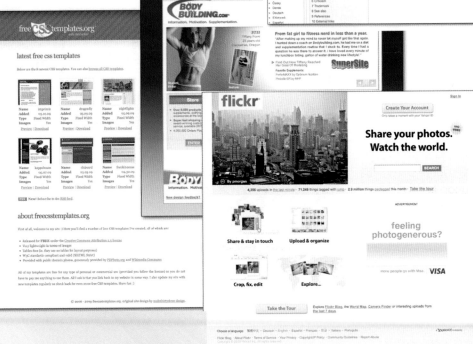

Tip 3: Do not get too clever

Clever web design is usually not usable web design. Nobody cares about your website's cleverness except perhaps other web designers and web design coffee-table books. When I get clever with web design the results are usually disastrous.

1 Review the Flash site templates throughout this book. Without exception, they are brilliant but not very usable for a typical website.

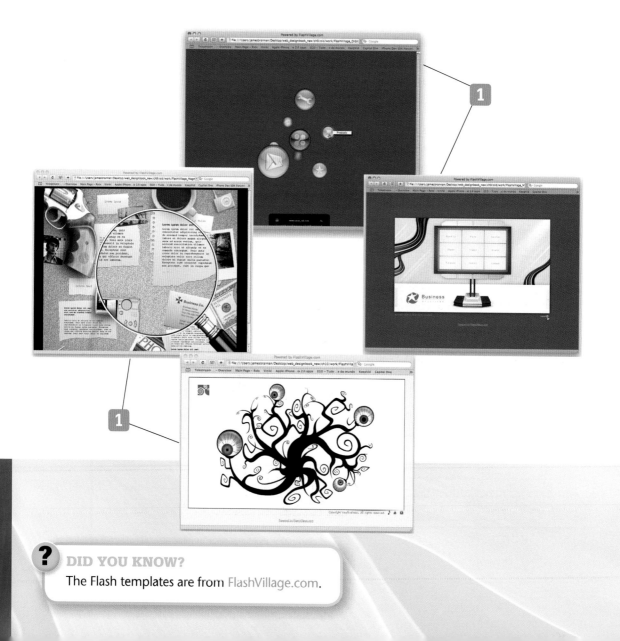

2 Here's a preview of several of my clever hypothetical webpages presented throughout this book. I think I am being clever, but in reality, I am simply making the pages less usable.

HOT TIP: Avoid eye candy. Eye candy consists of elements such as JavaScript clocks, menus with special effects, and other assorted nonfunctional additions to your website.

Tip 4: Usability is paramount

This tip is actually many combined into one. Remember usability is paramount. If a user cannot use your site, he or she will leave it. These steps, previewed here, are discussed in more detail later in this book.

1. Remember to use relative fonts, not fixed fonts.

2. Use a liquid layout to accommodate browser size variation.

3. Ensure visited links are a different colour than non-visited links.

4. Be certain images enhance your site's message and are not mere decorations.

5. Ensure users can scan your webpages by using headings and chunking your information.

6. Ensure your site is accessible for users with disabilities by including features such as alt tags for images.

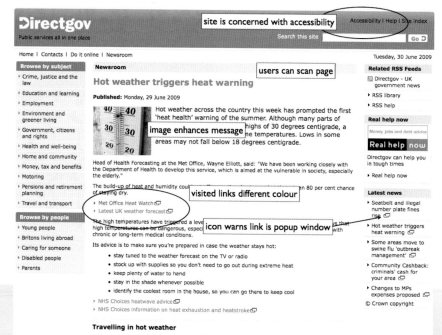

Tip 5: The Web is an easily changeable medium

When faced with all the steps presented in this book, you might get overwhelmed. But don't; webpages, unlike traditional software, are easily updatable. You can publish your webpages before being complete and you can easily update them once published. So don't be afraid to make mistakes, they are easily corrected.

1 Realise this tip is not advocating 'under-construction' pages (see Chapter 2), but rather, is simply reminding you that a website does not require being 100 per cent complete before being published. The example below shows a tutorial website released before finishing tutorials.

2 It is often said that the final 10 per cent of a software project usually accounts for 90 per cent of the effort. If you wait until your site is 100 per cent complete, then there is a probability it will never be published. Once you publish your site, you have a greater incentive to finish it, particularly if you start getting positive feedback from users.

Tip 6: Nobody reads webpages: write succinctly and use ample headers and subheaders

In this book you will find this tip expanded upon in Chapter 3. You should use short information chunks, write like a journalist, and use ample headings and subheadings. Journalists present the most important information at a story's beginning. Headings and subheadings help users ascertain a paragraph's topic without actually reading the chapter. All of these tips help 'skim-reading' users determine your webpage's content without actually having to read the entire page in detail.

1. Navigate to the Directgov website (www.direct.gov.uk). Navigate to one of the numerous articles on the site.

2. For instance, the page illustrated here provides information for Britons who will be living abroad.

3. Notice the page has ample headers and subheaders.

4. The page presents the information in small information chunks that are easily read.

5. The page also provides links to more detailed information should a user desire more information on a topic.

6. Notice that without reading the page you can ascertain that the page contains information on moving to the European Union and taxes, pensions, and benefits when abroad. You gain all this information by merely scanning the headers.

Tip 7: Check your work

You should always test your site. A site with spelling mistakes and incorrect grammar is not a convincing site. Check your site's grammar and spelling. A site with broken hyperlinks, missing images and other mistakes also results in an unprofessional site. Chapter 10 covers this tip in more detail.

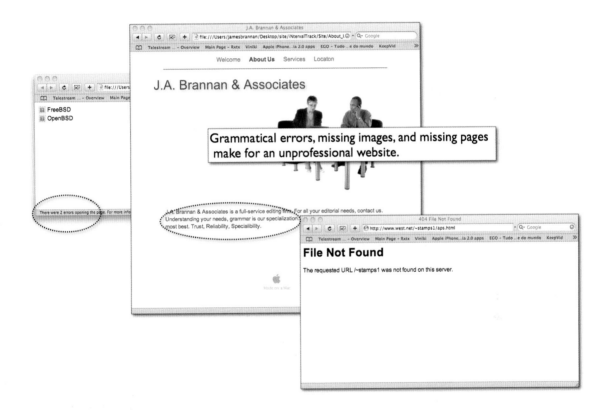

Grammatical errors, missing images, and missing pages make for an unprofessional website.

Tip 8: Be consistent

Consistency is as important as having a well thought out, accurate site. Maintain the same look and feel, and navigation strategy, throughout the site. This tip will become more apparent as you progress through this book.

1 Navigate to www.wtopnews.com, a Washington D.C. news organisation's online version of its news radio station.

2 Navigate through the site and notice that it maintains consistency from page to page.

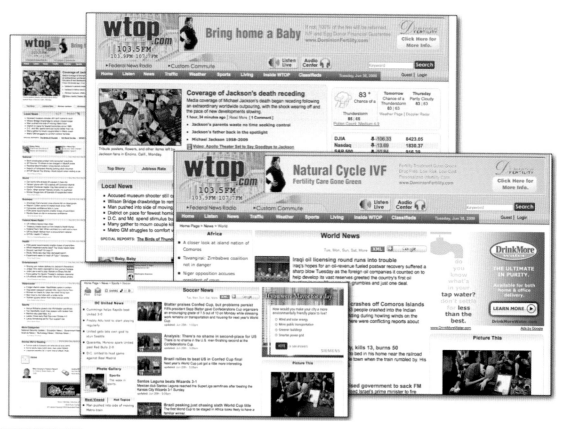

Tip 9: Don't forget your users, all of them

The Internet is a vital information source for people around the world. If possible, do not exclude a group because of a disability.

1 Navigate to the Directgov website (www.direct.gov.uk) and notice the Accessibility link in the upper right corner.

2 Click the link and your browser loads a page where the site explains how it makes itself more accessible to all.

3 The site tries to accommodate a wide browser variety, both current and outdated.

4 The site also tries to accommodate disabled users.

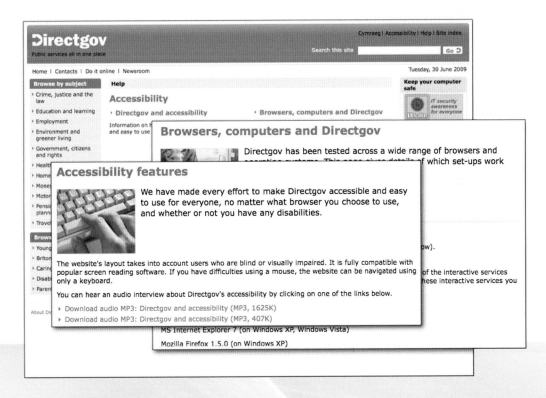

Tip 10: Remember, web design is supposed to be fun

If you do not enjoy web design, then chances are your website will not be very good. In that case, consider hiring someone to do it for you. There are many amateur and professional web designers who can develop your site relatively cheaply.

1 Navigate to craigslist.org. This website is a good place to obtain less experienced web designers who are eager to gain more experience. Be careful, though; protect yourself, as it is a classified ad service.

2 If you do enjoy web design, then consider pursuing it as a career. Web design does not require a computer science degree nor does it require an art degree. While both these backgrounds help, they are no substitute for training and practical experience. There is no school I know of that teaches how to write computer books. Experience with computers, college writing experience, desire and perseverance are all that is required. The same is true for web design.

craigslist uk — london w

1 Planning your website

Introduction

Before developing a site, you should plan. Plan what you wish accomplishing by creating a web site. After knowing what you or your client wishes accomplishing, you then brainstorm what service you might offer a user. Successful sites offer services to its users.

Review several sites' services and self-interested goals

Providing services to a user population brings the desired users to your site and keeps them coming back. But you must also have a clear understanding of your goals, and tailor the services your site offers so it fulfils your goals.

1 Navigate to each site listed in Table 1.1 and review each one.

2 Notice the service each site offers.

3 Now notice the self-interested goals each site fulfils for each site's owners.

HOT TIP: Review competitors' websites. Assess what they did poorly and what they did well. Avoid your competitors' mistakes and copy their successes.

Table 1.1 Services offered by several sites and how the services meet the owner's goals

Site	Service offered	Self-interest goals
www.freecss templates.org	Offers free CSS templates.	Provides a link to paid templates and sells advertising. Provides a creative outlet for template author's energy.
www.bodybuilding.com	Provides an extensive exercise database. Provides thousands of training articles. Provides an extensive user forum to share information on exercise topics.	Has positioned itself as the leading online retailer to buy nutrition supplements.
www.google.com	Provides the best search engine on the Internet.	Sells advertising.
www.flickr.com	Provides a central location where photographers can share their art.	Sells advertising. Allows users to upgrade to paid membership for premium services.
www.risawn.com/ blogger.html	Provides a blog where readers can waste time and vicariously read about someone else's life. Allows a user to post opinions to her posts.	Provides a cathartic release for her creative energy. Her day job is a US Army Drill Sergeant, which probably does not allow her to explore her creative side. Allows her an international audience for her political and personal beliefs.
www.rosie.com	Provides a blog where readers can read about one of their favourite media personalities. Allows direct communication with Rosie through her askrosie section.	Provides a cathartic release for her opinions and thoughts, uncensored by the media. Provides a way to promote her charities and things she thinks are important.
www.direct.gov.uk	Provides a central information clearinghouse on everything related to the UK government.	Makes government services easier for the public. This makes the agency's job easier, and puts the agency under less scrutiny.
www.bikeman.com	Provides an extensive bicycle parts catalogue and related accessories.	Makes the retailer a leading location for an online shopper, as they know what they need can probably be found on this site.

Determine your site's purpose

After deciding to build a website, the first thing you should do is determine the site's purpose. What are its goals? What are your goals? Do the site's goals and your goals complement each other? Are the goals the same?

1 Determine your goals (or your client's goals). For instance, suppose you are developing the product shown here.

2 Write the goals down, in order, and refine the list. These are the goals for a website I wish to develop to promote my hypothetical product and my writing.

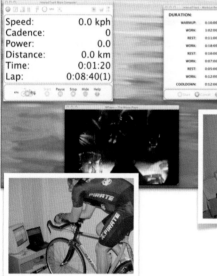

ALERT: The goals are your goals. The goals are not hypothetical user goals, those goals come later. You need to be clear about what you want your site to do for you.

Site goals:

1. Give away freeware product on the internet.

2. Promote programming abilities.

3. Obtain new consulting business.

4. Promote books.

5. Obtain new book contracts.

ALERT: Be careful you do not get analysis paralysis. Do not try defining too many goals in too much detail. Keep it high level. Try limiting your goals to 10 at most.

HOT TIP: Do not assume you already know your goals. I am an automaton, I often do things without knowing why, and chances are you do too.

Narrow your purpose to one goal

Although this step might seem superficial, it helps you focus on your single most important goal. You should have a single, clear goal before design.

1 Condense your goals into one main goal.

2 Consider whether the goal is sufficiently concrete and at the right level. For instance, if your goal is 'to create a personal webpage' you gain little insight into your true goal as this goal is too wide-ranging. Cut through the rhetoric and find the true goal.

3 Navigate to www.nationalpriorities.org and notice the site's goal. 'National Priorities Project analyzes and clarifies federal data so that people can understand and influence how their tax dollars are spent.' The site (and the organisation) has one goal: informing US taxpayers how the government is spending their money.

HOT TIP: Make the website's goal sufficiently detailed so that it has a clear meaning and purpose.

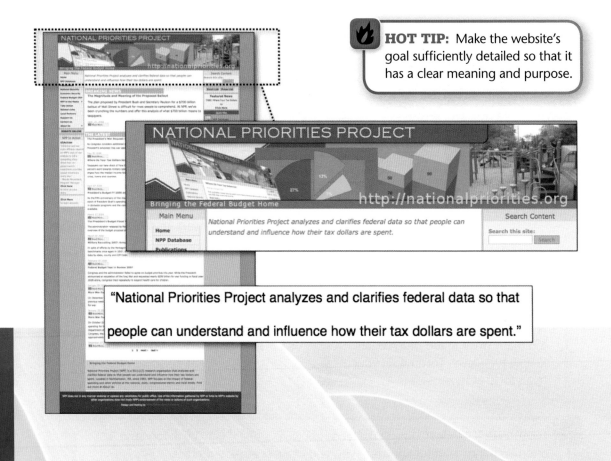

"National Priorities Project analyzes and clarifies federal data so that people can understand and influence how their tax dollars are spent."

Identify your target audience

Every website has a target audience. Some sites have a narrow audience while others have a wider one. Understand the different visitors you wish to attract to your site.

Some questions for considering a site's potential audience include the following:

- How many different visitor types (groups) will the site attract?

- What are each group's characteristics?

- Are there any potential roadblocks that prevent reaching your goals with a particular group? For instance, is your product too expensive? Is a large group segment visually impaired? Is a group's primary language not English?

- Why should each group visit your site?

- What are each group's favourite sites?

- How different or similar is each group?

- Do you need to narrow your appeal to fewer groups?

1. Consider your site's primary users.

2. Consider other users that might visit your site.

3. Remember, all this book's remaining chapters must be considered in light of your target audience.

4. Consider the DirectgovKids website's target users are children so the site's design reflects this audience.

5. Broaden your consideration to other, less important users than your primary user.

6. The DirectgovKids website's secondary users are teachers and parents. Although similar, in the teachers' area the site tailors its design towards teachers and parents.

Teachers' area

FAQs

HTML Teachers' area

Enter World

Campaigns

Welcome to the Teachers' Area of the DirectgovKids website. It is designed to offer help and support as you explore the DirectgovKids world with your students. The site contains all sorts of resources: games, animations, slideshows, factfiles and video clips. A range of themes are covered, including keeping fit and healthy, staying safe, caring for the environment, voting and democracy, and exploring your local community. The lesson plans below are full of teaching ideas and show how the site can support you as you teach the primary curriculum.

Shine - celebrating the talent in everyone! Click here for more information.

SWINE FLU INFORMATION
0800 1 513 513
www.nhs.co.uk
www.direct.gov.uk/swineflu

Sites we like

Find out more about:
Democracy
Healthy eating
Animals
Exercise
Internet safety
Fire safety
Citizenship

Lesson Plans		Games & Animations	Instructions & Factfiles

There are many lesson plans on the DirectgovKids site. Use the drop-down menus to choose the topic, subject and key stage that are most relevant to you.

All Themes | All Subjects | KS

Who helps us to run our school?	Behaviour & Community	ICT, PSHE, Citizenship, English	①
How do schools work?	Behaviour & Community	ICT, PSHE, Citizenship, Geography	②
What do pets need?	Behaviour & Community	PSHE, Citizenship, Science	①
Naming a police dog	Behaviour & Community	ICT, PSHE, Citizenship, Maths	②

DirectgovKids

ALERT: All sites have a 'casual user', the casual surfer who stumbles upon your site. Always ask yourself how important this user is. Remember, you can't please everyone, all the time.

Have a call to action

Brian and Jeffrey Eisenberg wrote a book entitled *Call to Action: Secret Formulas to Improve Online Success*. In it, they discuss having a call to action. Key to any site's success is persuasion. If your site persuades a user to do what you wish them to do, then your site is a success. Key to persuasion is having a call to action.

1   Navigate to Survival International's website (www.survival-international.org).

2   Note that the content below the banner has several clear calls to action. Here is the site shown on 10 October 2008. Notice the message 'The Enawene Nawe need you', which is blatant, as it is urgent and time sensitive.

3   Notice the message, 'Bruce Parry Teams up with Music World's Brightest Stars for "Survival" Album'. The message is subtle as it promotes an album, and is not trying to save a tribe's existence.

? DID YOU KNOW?
A call to action can be subtle or blatant.

4 Now notice the hypothetical store site which is a free CSS template by CSSCreme. com. The site has no explicit call to action, but the implicit call to action is clear: buy a tool.

HOT TIP: A site can have several calls to actions. Be careful they do not conflict or obscure one another.

Understand your constraints

You should understand your constraints early in a project. Not understanding your contraints is the largest risk to not completing your website.

1 Consider how much money you have. What is your budget?

2 Consider how much time you have. How long can you take? Even if the project is you creating your homepage, you have constraints. You have a job, hobbies, and maybe a few kids. Time spent working on your web site is time taken from other activities. You only have so much time in any given day, so you have constraints.

3 Write down your constraints and refer to them often. Use these constraints to remind you that your site must have limits.

4 Use your constraints to plan how you will build your site. For instance, I was under tight time constraints to complete my site (my real site, not the hypothetical one scattered throughout this book), and so I opted to use the Endless CSS template from FreeCSSTemplates.com for my website and the Reference WordPress blog template from FreeWPThemes.net.

5 You must also consider monthly maintenance costs. Updating a site costs time and money. Because I wish to minimise the time required to update my site, I opted for a WordPress blog for posting new content, as WordPress makes updating my blog extremely easy.

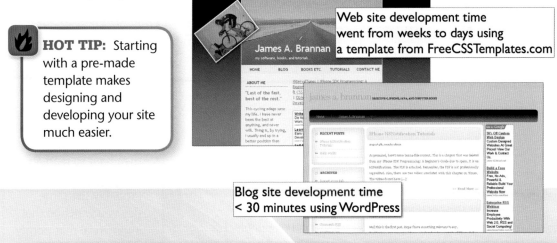

Web site development time went from weeks to days using a template from FreeCSSTemplates.com

Blog site development time < 30 minutes using WordPress

HOT TIP: Starting with a pre-made template makes designing and developing your site much easier.

HOT TIP: Knowing your constraints helps avoid scope creep. Scope creep is when extra features find their way into your product. It is characterised by "just one more page" or "just one more feature". Over time, these added features cause budget and time overruns, and usually cause projects to fail.

Identify a service you can offer users

If you want a really successful site, you need a real service your site can offer its users. Moreover, you need a service that will keep users coming back.

1 Consider how your site can offer a true service.

2 Can your site provide a tangible product like software, documentation, or information not easily obtained elsewhere?

3 After determining one or more services, brainstorm: is there a bigger, more valuable service you can offer?

4 Consider adding a user forum where users can share information and create a community out of your site: one example is bodybuilding.com's user forum.

ALERT: Do not forget your constraints. Providing services costs time and money.

HOT TIP: A service is not creating an online magazine that simply promotes your agenda. When was the last time you went to an ecommerce merchant to read an 'informative magazine'? Probably the same day you watched that infomercial that poorly disguised itself as free financial advice. Did you believe it? So if you are not gullible, why believe your users are?

? DID YOU KNOW?

Do not let this section discourage you. Your site can offer small services that make it much more valuable. For instance, if developing a website for your church, services you might provide include clear directions and a map to your location, a services schedule, contact information and an event calendar. These services, albeit humble, should be what you focus on while designing your site.

Make sure your ecommerce site offers a service

Successful ecommerce sites usually fill a niche market, selling items hard to obtain at a traditional brick-and-mortar shop. Successful ecommerce sites might sell items much more cheaply than traditional shops, or offer a greater selection. To compete on the Web, your ecommerce site must offer a service to users.

1 Consider www.bikeman.com. If you need a bicycle part, the site probably has it and can ship it within a couple days.

2 Notice how many bicycle wheels are offered for sale. For instance, there are over 190 different bicycle wheel sets. Moreover, the site carries less expensive bicycle parts; parts so inexpensive many retailers don't want to bother with them. Bikeman is offering a service through its bicycle parts selection.

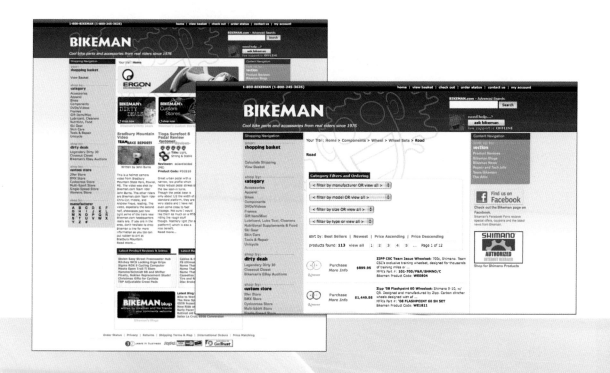

3 Now consider AnimeNation. This site offers anime videos and magazines to anime enthusiasts. You are not required to offer the most extensive selection in a category. If you fulfil a niche market, you too can have a successful ecommerce site.

When offering a service, be careful it is not shallow

Take care to not offer shallow, self-serving services. Your users will recognise this shallowness immediately.

1. The JamesSpeak hypothetical site illustrates an extremely shallow service. All the site's supposed advice on audio speakers is a sales pitch for the speakers sold through the site.

2 Contrast this with Bodybuilding.com, an ecommerce site that sells nutritional supplements. Notice the extensive articles, forum, exercise database and other features.

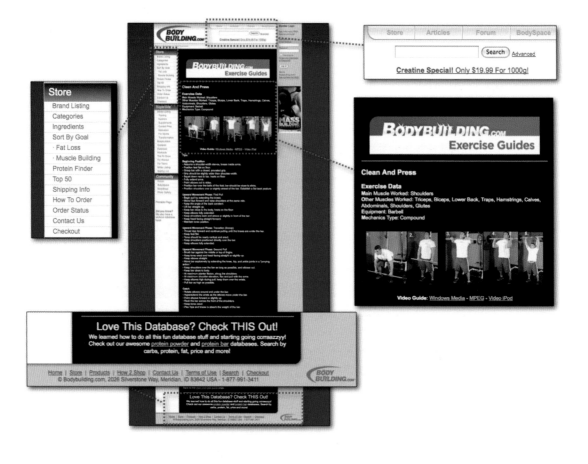

Gather requirements, even if you don't think there are any

After knowing your site's primary mission, and the services it is to provide, you should formalise those services into requirements. A requirement is a statement that identifies a necessary feature your site must have. These statements direct how you design and develop your site.

1 Write your requirements in a list. Suppose, after analysing what I wish to accomplish with my personal website, I write the requirements listed in Table 1.2. Writing requirements for a small site might seem excessive, but it is not.

2 Compare your requirements list against your goals and the services you wish to offer users.

3 Desires formalised into requirements become website pages. And as you will learn in Chapter 10, these requirements provide tests that you use to ensure your website does what you want it to do.

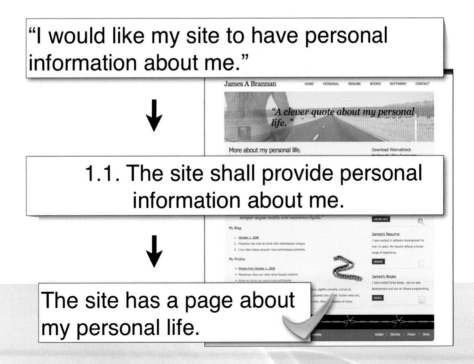

"I would like my site to have personal information about me."

1.1. The site shall provide personal information about me.

The site has a page about my personal life.

Table 1.2

1	The site shall provide personal information about me.
1.2	The site shall provide a blog.
1.3	The site shall provide photos.
2	The site shall provide a summary of my books.
2.1	The site shall provide a means for users to buy my books.
3	The site shall provide a summary of my software written.
4	The site shall provide online help for my freeware, iNtervalTrack.
5	The site shall provide my resumé.
6	The site shall provide a means to download iNtervalTrack.
6.1	The site shall require users to register and agree with iNtervalTrack's licence.
7	The site shall use HTML and CSS to present its content.
8	The site shall save user information of users who register for software.

DID YOU KNOW?

Software engineers call this formalisation step requirements analysis. Requirements analysis's goal is to gather the functions software must provide if the software is to meet user needs. This step could be formal, or informal, depending upon the project's size.

HOT TIP: By writing down requirements, you know exactly what features your site must provide.

Create a use case diagram

A good way to capture user requirements is through a use case diagram. A use case diagram is part of the Unified Modelling Language (UML). Software engineers use UML to design a software system before developing and writing the actual software.

1. Identify your users and add them to this diagram as stick figures.

2. Write the primary activities users perform on your site as use cases.

3. Determine optional activities that extend the primary activities; these activities extend a use case.

4. Determine the sub-activities users must perform to meet a primary activity. These activities are included by the primary activities.

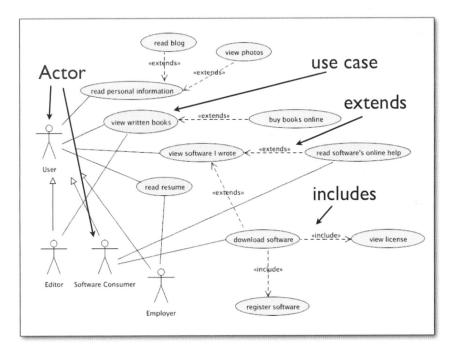

> **ALERT:** This chapter's use cases are simple. Often use cases involve more extended use cases. For these situations, it helps to list the use cases in numbered steps on paper prior to creating a use case diagram. Refer to any book on UML for more details on use case analysis.

WHAT DOES THIS MEAN?

Google: To conduct an Internet search on a topic or person.

Service: A service is a useful feature, or utility, provided to a site's users. For instance, Flickr offers users a service by allowing them to share photos with one another. Or Wikipedia offers a service to users with its online dictionary.

Blog: A website where an individual regularly posts commentary and other material. The online equivalent to a combined journal and scrapbook.

Serial port: A serial communication interface on a computer where information is transmitted to a computer through a cable. USB ports have largely replaced serial ports, but serial port to USB converters that mimic a serial port are still available.

Ecommerce: Buying and selling goods over the Internet. A contraction of the words electronic and commerce.

CSS template: A predesigned cascading style sheet that a designer can download and use as the basis for his or her site.

Cascading Style Sheet (CSS): A design language used by webpages to format its content.

Brick-and-mortar: Web vernacular for a retail establishment which has a physical presence rather than being solely online. Your local high street shops are brick-and-mortar stores.

Web 2.0: Web vernacular for sites which offer user interactive services, where the user is part of a community. For instance, Flickr (www.flickr.com) and YouTube (www.youtube.com) are considered Web 2.0 sites.

? DID YOU KNOW?

Use case diagrams graphically model the results of use case analysis. Use case analysis is similar to requirements analysis, but more specialised. Use cases capture user interaction with the system. The user is called an actor and the user's interaction is called a use case.

2 Website architecture

Introduction

After you have a concrete idea about the website you are to build, you create the site's architecture. Start with a blueprint based upon the activities determined in Chapter 1. The blueprints form the site's skeleton or framework. Upon this framework, you later design your site's webpages. This chapter has six primary steps for creating your website architecture. The remaining tasks are best practices to remember while performing these six primary steps shown in the diagram.

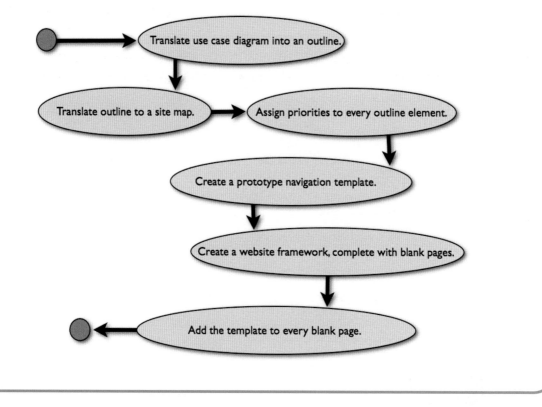

Translate the use case diagram into an outline

The first thing you should do after formalising your use cases is to translate the use case diagram into an outline. Having an outline helps organise the use cases into a logical hierarchy.

1 Create a top-level outline (as shown here) from the use case diagram on page 31.

2 Create a second level from the use cases that extend or include the primary use cases.

3 Add email to the outline's top level, as although the figure on page 31 omits email, every site should have a method to contact its owner.

4 Downloading software involves accepting the licence, registering, and then physically downloading the software. Make these three use cases third-level topics.

> A. About Me (Personal)
>   1. My Blog
>   2. View Photos
> B. Books I've Written
>   1. Buy Online
> C. Resume
> D. Software I've Written
>   1. Online Help
>   2. Download Software
>   a. License Agreement
>   b. Register
>   c. Download
> E. Email me

ALERT: Most use cases translate directly to an HTML page, but a few do not. There are no steadfast rules, so use your best judgement.

Assign priorities to every outline element

After translating the use cases into an outline, assign priorities to each outline element. Assigning priorities helps determine an outline's most important topics (pages).

1 Look at the example here. It is important that people can download my software easily. I also want to give employers easy access to my resumé and editors easy access to my written books. And of course I want potential employers and editors with book contracts to contact me, so emailing me is of utmost importance.

2 Assign 'Email Me' a priority of 1. Assign 'Download Software', 'Books I've Written', and 'Resumé' a priority of 1.

3 Discussing my software and my personal information is not so important to me. Assign 'Software I've Written' a priority of 2 and 'About Me' a priority of 3. Because it's not important if users read my blog or view my photos, assign 'My Blog' and 'View Photos' a priority of 3.

4 Downloading software is a linear, three-step process. A user must agree to the licence, register and then download the software. Moreover, he or she must perform these three steps in order, without skipping a step. So these are sub-steps of the Download Software topic. Assign these three sub-steps a priority of 1.

```
A. About Me (Personal) 3
    1. My Blog 3
    2. View Photos 3
B. Books I've Written 1
    1. Buy Online 2
C. Resume 1
D. Software I've Written 2
    1. Online Help 1
    2. Download Software 1
        a. License Agreement 1
        b. Register 1
        c. Download 1
E. Email me 1
```

Translate the outline to a site map

The outline translates into your site map. A site map is a visual model of a website's pages. The site map should follow the outline's structure.

1 Refer to the sample outline on the previous page. Create a top-level page, My Homepage.

2 Create first-level pages from the top-level topics shown on the previous page. Feel free to change the names.

3 Create second-level pages.

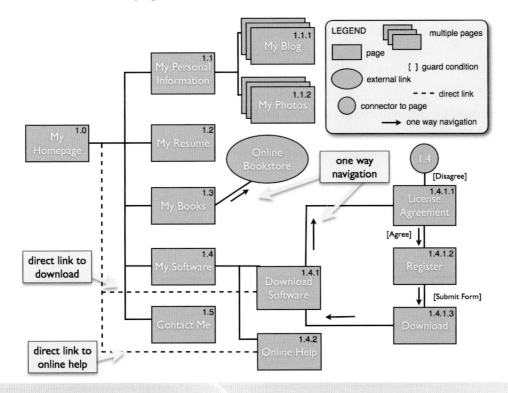

HOT TIP: Number your pages. Referring to a page using a number is easier than referring to a page by its name.

4 Create third-level pages. Note that downloading is a three-step process. First, a user must agree to the licence. Second, a user must register his or her name and email address and then submit this information. Third, the user must click on a direct link to the software's installer. A user must perform this three-step process sequentially, without skipping a step. Indicate this sequential navigation using arrows to show the one-way flow.

5 A user must agree to the licence. Show this required agreement using what is called a guard condition between the 1.4.1.1 and 1.4.1.2 pages. If a user disagrees, the site should return the user to the 1.4 page.

6 Buying one of my books online requires sending a user to an external bookseller such as Amazon, so indicate Online Bookstore as an external link.

7 My blog and photos are topics that will probably grow over time. As they grow, I will probably add new pages. Show these pages' multi-page nature by using multiple pages in the site map.

ALERT: If your site map is not immediately intuitive, be certain to include a legend explaining all symbols.

HOT TIP: Pages that are important, yet two or three levels deep in the outline, should have direct links on the top-level home page (see 'Follow the three-click rule', next). For instance, as illustrated on page 36, allowing users to download my software, access online help, and view my resumé is of utmost importance. But only my resumé is a top-level outline element and so the other two elements become direct links, bypassing the site's page hierarchy.

Follow the three-click rule

When designing your site's outline and subsequent site map, remember, users are impatient. If a user cannot find the desired information quickly, he or she will usually look elsewhere. That 'elsewhere' is usually a competitor's site. The three-click rule states that users should never have to click more than three links to reach the desired information.

1. Consider the US government's Internal Revenue Service (IRS) website (www.irs.gov). The three things most Americans want from this site are finding out their tax refund status, printing a form to pay their taxes, and paying taxes electronically.

2. Suppose you were an American who wanted to find your refund status. Click the 'Where's My Refund?' hyperlink. This is the first click.

3. Scan the instructions page, and find the 'Where's My Refund?' hyperlink and click it. Note that the IRS purposely hid the link to try to get you to read the page. Chances are, though, if you are like me, you just skimmed it until you found the link.

4. Review the form, but do not bother submitting it. Had you submitted it, clicking the Submit button would have been the third click.

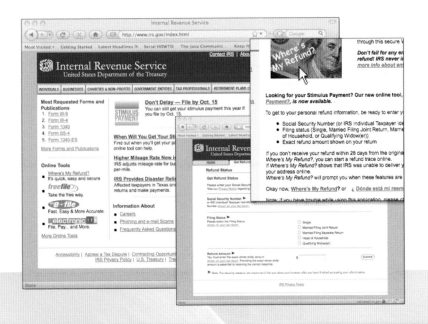

SEE ALSO: Not everything can be three clicks. This is where Chapter 1's "Narrow your purpose to one goal" and "Have a call to action" best practices are relevant. Be certain that pages most relevant to your site's main goal and pages relevant to what actions you wish users to take are never more than three clicks away.

Use sequential navigation when appropriate

Use sequential navigation when you have a series of pages with equivalent importance on the same topic. These pages follow a linear path. Pages in a book's chapter are sequential, as are most magazine articles. You move from page to page, sequentially turning the page from page n to page n+1.

1 This diagram illustrates sequential page navigation.

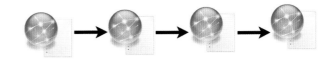

2 Navigate to freecsstemplates. org and navigate through the templates.

3 Note that you are navigating sequentially between pages of templates.

4 Try finding another site that uses sequential navigation. Hint: Google's search results are sequential, as are Flickr's.

Use external links sparingly and prudently

Have you ever visited a site where seemingly every other word is linked to an external site? External links take a user away from your site and throws him or her into a foreign site, causing confusion and frustration.

1 Navigate to JavaWorld's website (www.javaworld.com) and find the article 'MapReduce programming with Apache Hadoop' by Ravi Shankar and Govindu Narendra.

2 Notice the article discusses an external resource, Apache Hadoop. The article links to Hadoop, but when you click the link, it takes you to an anchor at the page's bottom. There you can choose to navigate to Apache Hadoop's site if you wish.

3 Click the external link and note that it opens in a new browser window.

4 Notice that the sponsored links are limited to separate areas on the webpage, not strewn throughout the page. All this helps to prevent distracting users away from the main site's content unless they specifically want to follow a link.

? DID YOU KNOW?

Throwing a user into a foreign site, like it or not, implies that the external site meets your approval.

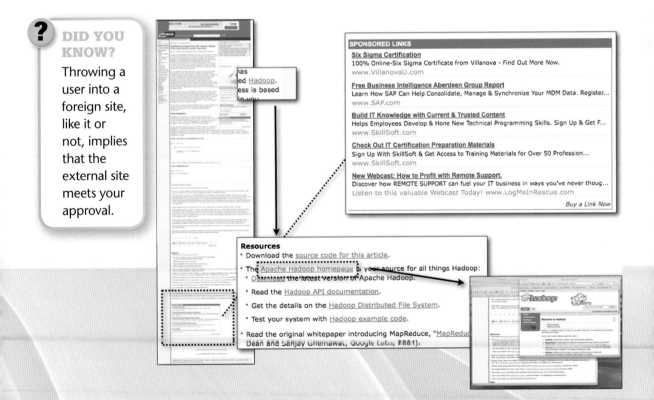

Do not let ads interfere with your site's content

Advertisers have scrambled to take part in Internet marketing, offering you untold monetary rewards for your participation as a web developer. But remember, the monetary compensation you will probably receive is slight compared with the potential angst you can cause your users. Go ahead and include ads, just do so with, so the ads do not detract too much from your site.

1 Navigate to www.fixedgearfever.com, an online source for bicycle racing on velodromes. Notice it contains a considerable number of advertisements.

2 Note the ads are confined to four locations, the left margin, the right margin, across the page's top (below the page's banner), and across the page's bottom (above the page's housekeeping links). Thus the ads do not detract from the site's content.

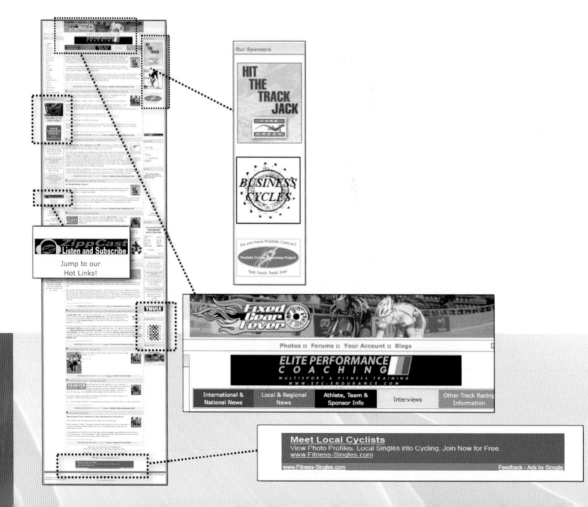

Ensure your site has no dead ends

A dead end is a page that provides no navigation links, making the page a dead end. The only way a user can navigate back to your site is through the browser's back button. When creating your site's framework, be certain not to create any dead ends.

1 Look at this hypothetical page. As well as being a brilliant design (yes, I am available for freelance design consultation), it also illustrates a dead end page.

2 Notice there are only two ways to escape: using your browser's back button or closing your browser window.

SEE ALSO: Refer to 'Ensure every page has a page header' and 'Ensure every page has a page footer' to avoid this problem entirely.

Do not use under construction pages

Often, developers publish a website before its completion. You really should not publish a site until it is completed, but if you must, then do not use an under construction page as a placeholder for the actual content to be completed. Instead, do not provide the link in the first place.

1 Navigate to www.google.com and enter the keywords 'under construction'.

2 Navigate to some of the sites. Note that government agencies, large and small businesses, non-profit organisations and personal home pages all commit this 'under construction' sin.

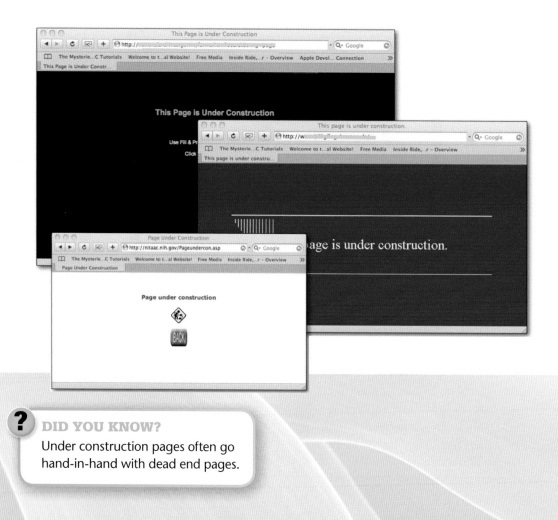

? DID YOU KNOW?

Under construction pages often go hand-in-hand with dead end pages.

Ensure every page says who, what, when and where

In college, journalism students learn that every story should tell the reader who, what, where, when, and why. A sixth tenet, sometimes added, is how. Like journalists, web designers, when developing a page, should ensure who, what, when and where are provided on every page. It lends credibility to your site, and makes it more professional.

1. Navigate to http://www.lewrockwell.com/gee/gee17.html and skim the content. I don't care if you believe the author's claims, I only half believe most.

2. Notice that Rick Gee wrote the article: it is clearly marked (who).

3. He wrote it for LewRockwell.com, and if you follow the link back to the main site, you quickly discover it is a website about American politics with a libertarian political leaning (where).

4. Scroll down the page and you see the date. Rick Gee wrote this page on February 26, 2002 (when).

SEE ALSO: Who, what, when and where are usually provided in a page's header and footer. See the sections on headers and footers in this chapter.

ALERT: Who, what, when and where not only applies to controversial political sites; sites such as Amazon and Google also provide this information, although on many sites who and where are often the same.

Ensure every page has a page header

A header is the area at the top of a webpage that usually identifies the site. It repeats on most, if not all, webpages across the site. It is the most important element a page has and is vital to creating a consistent site.

1 Navigate to www.wtopnews.com, a local Washington, D.C. news radio station's website.

2 Note that the logo is within the first four inches of the top left corner. The header contains a navigation bar, a search bar, and links for users to listen live on the Internet.

3 Navigate through the site; the same header repeats across the site.

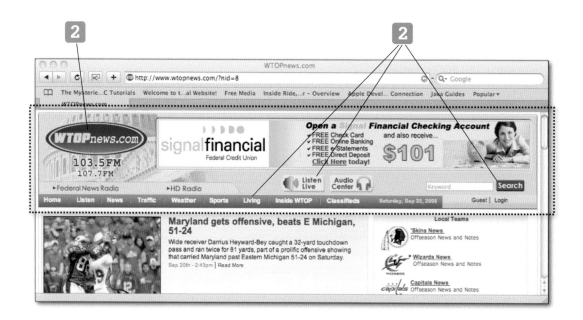

? DID YOU KNOW?

Experts recommend that within the first four inches of a page's top left corner you place something indicating your identity.

4 However, no design rule is absolute. Navigate to the Department of Health's website (www.dh.gov.uk). The Department of Health varies its header, depending upon the page. But the variation is slight, and the header remains consistent, despite the text and image change.

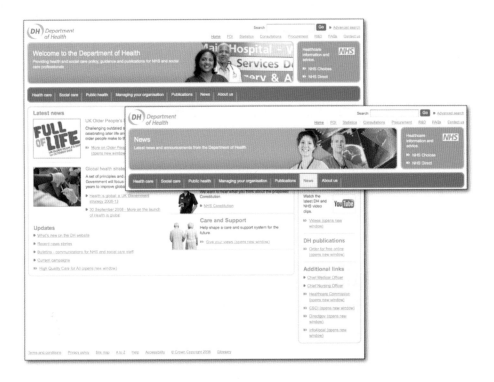

ALERT: Headers create consistency and usability for users; before modifying the header on different pages, ask if the modification is truly necessary and actually provides navigation context.

Ensure every page has a page footer

Almost as important as the header is the footer, and like the header, the footer should repeat on every page. Footers usually contain "housekeeping" links to topics such as the site map, terms of site use, copyright and similar topics. The footer also commonly contains information such as last updated, contact information, and sometimes the site's top-level navigation categories.

1 Navigate to the UK government's Department for Culture, Media, and Sport homepage (www.culture.gov.uk).

2 Scroll to the page's bottom and notice the footer. Navigate to a couple of the site's internal pages; note the footer is consistent across pages.

Make hyperlinks and icons explicit

You have probably been to at least one website where the navigation was confusing. An easy way to confuse users is by designing navigation links that do not look like hyperlinks.

1 Refer to the two hypothetical pages shown here. Besides being design masterpieces, complete with a scantily clad model, they illustrate ambiguous and explicit icon links.

2 Note that in the first version, although the graphics look like they might be links, until you move your mouse over an icon this is not completely clear.

3 In the second version, the page labels all the graphics with a text hyperlink, allowing you to click the graphic or the text link.

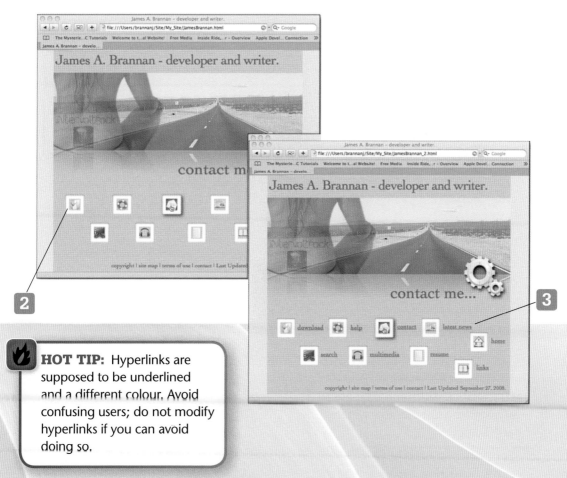

HOT TIP: Hyperlinks are supposed to be underlined and a different colour. Avoid confusing users; do not modify hyperlinks if you can avoid doing so.

Use breadcrumb trails when designing complex sites

Breadcrumb trails show a user's location within a site. A breadcrumb trail is a single line of text links that traces the path from a website's home to the current page. Each level is a link to the relevant page. The current page is usually not a link in the breadcrumb trail.

1 Refer to the hypothetical page shown here. The current page is electronic podcasts. This page is three levels deep from the home page.

2 Each hyperlink in the breadcrumb trail is a hyperlink to the level's main page. For instance, clicking podcasts would take you to a page listing podcasts.

3 Navigate to www.wtopnews.com, navigate through the site, and note its consistent breadcrumb use.

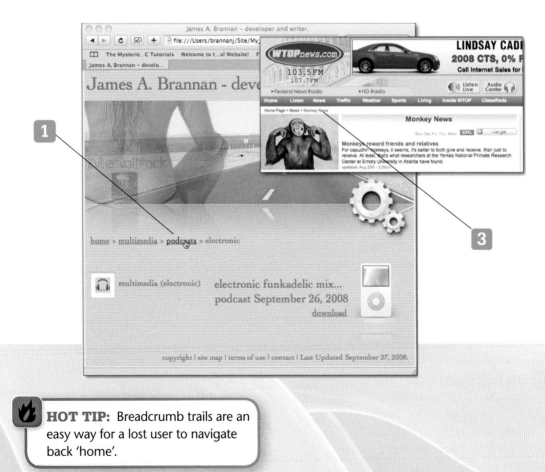

HOT TIP: Breadcrumb trails are an easy way for a lost user to navigate back 'home'.

Always create a site map or site index

If your site is more than a few pages, a site map is one of your site's most important pages. A site map lists your entire site's links on one page. If developing a larger site, consider using an alphabetised site index rather than a site map.

1 Navigate to www.nhsdirect.wales.nhs.uk and find its site map.

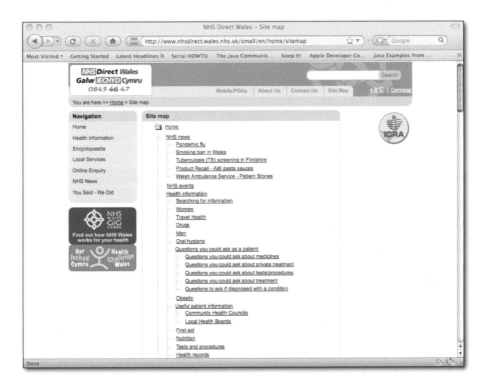

2 Navigate to www.direct.gov.uk and find its site index.

3 Note the similarities and differences between the two. Consider which one's style would be more appropriate for your site.

SEE ALSO: See 'Translate the outline to a site map' on page 37. This site map translates almost directly to the site map you created when first drafting your site, with the subsequent additions and subtractions accounted for.

? DID YOU KNOW?
A site index is exactly like a book's index, only each index term is a hyperlink to the site's relevant page.

Create a prototype navigation template

It is often helpful to create a prototype navigation template while still developing a site's architecture. Clients are impatient and want to see results immediately. And most clients do not consider site map results; they consider webpage results.

1 Navigate to www.freetemplates.org and find the Puzzled CSS template. I base the navigation template shown here on that template.

2 When creating a template, translate the first-level pages into your main navigation menu. Because the names in the map on page 37 are too long, I shortened them when adding them to the template.

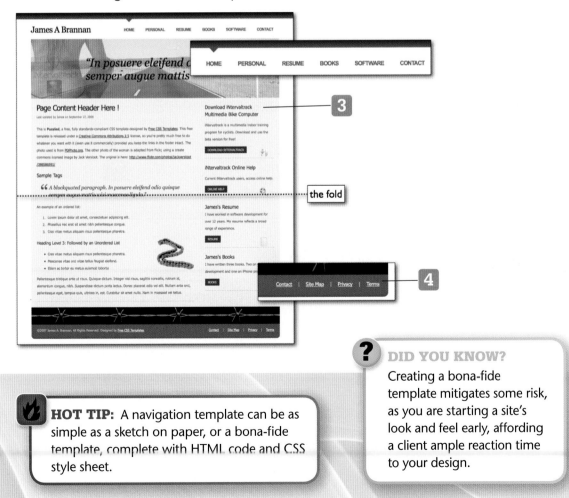

? **DID YOU KNOW?**
Creating a bona-fide template mitigates some risk, as you are starting a site's look and feel early, affording a client ample reaction time to your design.

HOT TIP: A navigation template can be as simple as a sketch on paper, or a bona-fide template, complete with HTML code and CSS style sheet.

3 Ensure the most important direct links make it onto your template. Downloading my software, accessing online help, reading my resumé, and reviewing my books are all important, so I modified the template's right column to include a short description and link for each important action. Every page's right column will repeat these four items.

4 I included 'housekeeping' links at the template's bottom. I added a link to contact me (email), a link to the site map, privacy policy, and terms for using my website.

5 Notice what the template lacks. It lacks a secondary navigation menu. A secondary navigation menu is for internal links and the Department of Health's secondary menu is shown here.

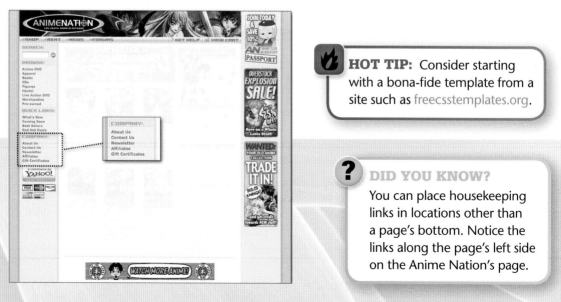

HOT TIP: Consider starting with a bona-fide template from a site such as freecsstemplates.org.

? DID YOU KNOW?

You can place housekeeping links in locations other than a page's bottom. Notice the links along the page's left side on the Anime Nation's page.

Create a website framework, complete with blank pages

Creating a website is challenging, akin to decorating your house. You arrange and rearrange until everything looks just right. Now, imagine you had to worry about building your house at the same time as you decorated it. Well, rather than building your website at the same time as you decorate it, why not build it first?

1 Create a framework of all the top-level pages in your site. Create a folder hierarchy to hold the site's pages and images.

2 Add dummy pages for every topic in your outline.

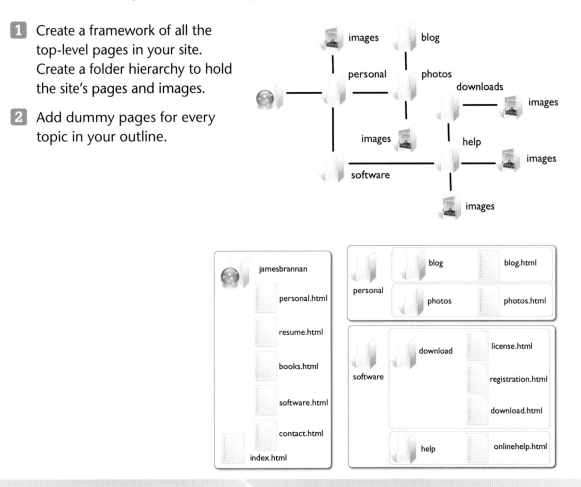

3 Add the template to every page, and fix the hyperlinks between every page. You then have a functioning site, albeit devoid of content. Now you can focus on decorating rather than building and decorating simultaneously.

3 Writing your text

Introduction

Vapid marketing brochures, no matter how well designed, do not garner users. They may gather design awards, but not users. Users desire services. Providing a service does not mean you must provide users with an application, though. Providing timely, informative information is an equally valuable service. But if the information is poorly written, it does not matter how timely and informative the information might be as people will just not read it.

Consider blogging if you enjoy writing

If you enjoy writing and are not afraid of sharing your life with an international audience, consider blogging. A blog is a website where a person enters his or her commentaries on various topics, much like a journal. Blogs also usually allow readers to post comments. This two-way discussion makes blogs an interactive communication medium.

1 Navigate to www.rosie.com. This is an example of a celebrity's blog.

2 Navigate to www.fatcyclist.com. This is an example of an individual's blog.

3 Navigate to blog.clearwriter.com. This is an example of a company's blog, where the blog provides a service, thus selling the company's services too.

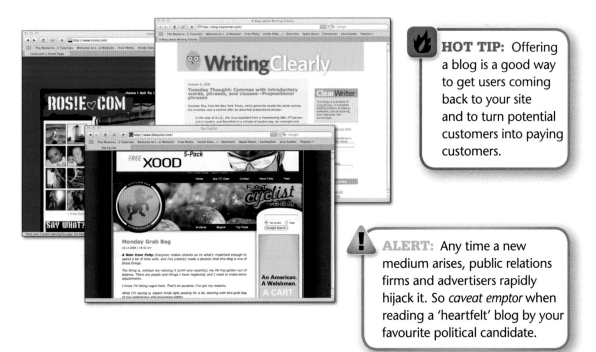

HOT TIP: Offering a blog is a good way to get users coming back to your site and to turn potential customers into paying customers.

ALERT: Any time a new medium arises, public relations firms and advertisers rapidly hijack it. So *caveat emptor* when reading a 'heartfelt' blog by your favourite political candidate.

ALERT: Blogging can be a big responsibility. It is hard work and emotionally draining. You must constantly share your thoughts and feelings, and respond to your readers. And some readers can be, well, idiots. Think twice before sharing your deepest secrets with an international audience and never divulge confidential information about your employers. People read blogs, and some will not be nice.

Ensure your site contains content

Despite what many graphic artists would have you believe, the Web is about text. I rarely go to websites to experience coolness. I bet you do not go to these cool sites either. Let these websites stay where they belong, in a full-colour book on your coffee table. Ensure your site contains content if you wish to attract and keep users.

1 Pick five sites, any sites, which you visit regularly.

2 Navigate to each in turn. Ask yourself, what is it about the site that draws you to it?

3 Review four sites I visit frequently, which are shown here. I visit all four for the service, or information, each provides. I visit these sites for textual information, not their design brilliance.

Chunk your information into bite-size pieces

Chunking information is a term that describes breaking information into small, easily read information chunks. Psychologists discovered that people tend to learn best by learning in discrete units, or chunks. Moreover, they discovered that seven, plus or minus two, chunks are the maximum that you should present per page.

1 Look at this diagram. Notice that there are nine chunks. Seven chunks is the optimal number of chunks according to psychologists.

2 Note that the chunks are not scattered haphazardly. You should organise chunks based upon similarity.

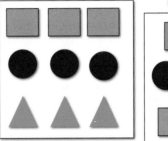
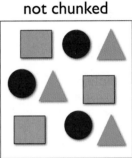

not chunked

chunked

3 Now look at the screenshot and notice how each story is a paragraph with a link to more information. By chunking information for users who browse, you allow them to access more comprehensive information if they want.

? DID YOU KNOW?

This page is a CSS template entitled 'Keep It Simple' and is available at www.styleshout.com.

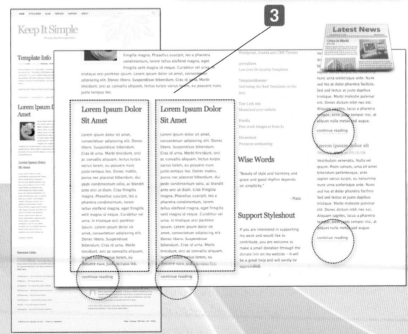

Write like a journalist

Journalists write using an inverted pyramid structure. The first few sentences are the most important. In these few sentences, you must tell the reader: who, what, when, where, why and how. After doing these six things, you can then tell the story in more depth. This writing style fits perfectly with web writing style.

1 Consider the template from the last section. The content is chunked. Each item on the page consists of one or two paragraphs, followed by a 'continue reading' link to more detailed content on other pages. Each chunk is sized to tell the reader who, what, when, where, why, and how quickly. If the user wishes more detail, he or she can click the link.

2 Notice the Featured column along the template's right side. The top paragraph is 61 words before linking to the 'continue reading' link.

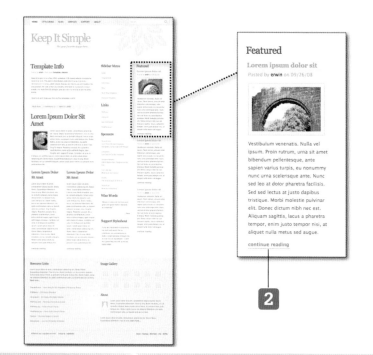

? DID YOU KNOW?

There are many other principles to journalistic writing, for instance, attributing sources and cutting extraneous words. However, the most important principle is that you write using an inverted pyramid.

3 Now navigate to WTOP News's website at www.wtopnews.com and then navigate to its local Maryland news section. Notice that the page's chunks are sized similarly to the Keep It Simple CSS template. Each new item's headline is a link to a more detailed story.

Write informative headings and subheadings

So, you followed the previous section's advice and wrote all your information in 50-word chunks with a hyperlink to the more detailed information. Many visitors will not even read those 50 words. You must write informative headings and subheadings for the users who skim.

1 Notice this hypothetical webpage (using the free TechJunkie CSS template by www. styleshout.com). The page summarises the story and provides a link for users who wish to continue reading. It also provides a subheader to pique a user's interest in the story. A user can easily skim the page and get a general understanding of its content.

2 Now notice the contents page. It uses headings and subheadings, and several callouts. Together the headings, subheadings and callouts provide a complete article summary. A skimmer can easily get the story's details without reading every word.

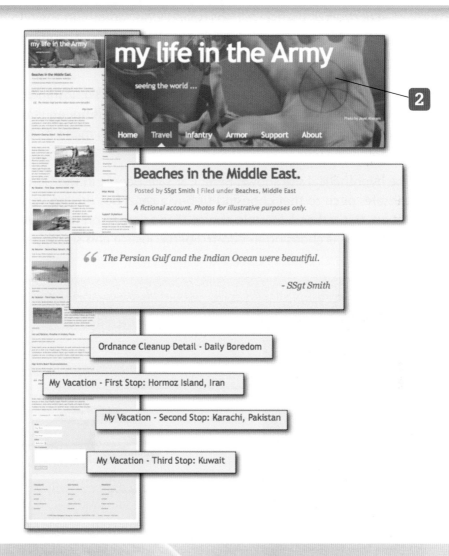

ALERT: Non-reading users are not stupid, nor are they shallow. They are busy. These users choose not to read, and no matter how enticing you make those 50 words, many will not read them.

HOT TIP: Callouts, a common technique in printed media, work well in web content.

Persuade users with subtle techniques

There are subtle techniques used every day by people trying to persuade us to take some course of action. Most people will not willingly do something they do not want to do. That is where persuasion comes in. Using subtle techniques, you can manipulate your site's users.

1 Frame your arguments so readers can empathise with you. For instance, suppose you are against the European Union. Frame the argument so it is not an independent UK versus European Union hegemony, but rather, the common man's freedom versus a vast European bureaucracy.

2 Refer to the hypothetical site shown here. Car salespeople in the USA commonly frame their sales pitch so that choosing to buy a car is not driving versus public transportation, but rather, a lifestyle choice. The salesperson tries making the buyer think that he or she is choosing freedom, liberty, justice and sex appeal.

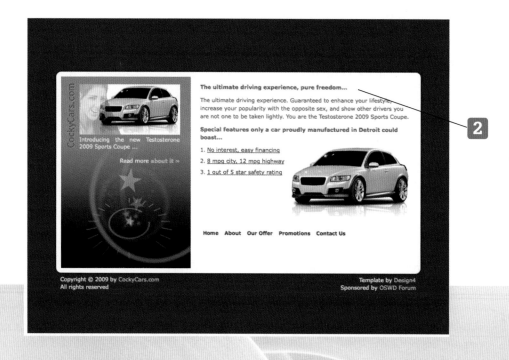

3 Consider persuading your site's users by providing a problem and a solution. State a problem up front. Remember most users only skim a webpage. You must grab their attention with a clear problem. After stating the problem, provide a solution. Of course, the solution just so happens to agree with the action you might wish users to take.

4 Remember to use an appropriate formality level. Choosing an appropriate formality level requires knowing your users. You must understand how formal you should or should not be. If trying to persuade someone to invest financially, you want a formal site that exudes confidence and professionalism. Choose an appropriate formality level for your message and your audience.

5 Consider persuading your users by empathising with them. Political candidates are masters at this technique. Despite usually being wealthy, most political candidates would seemingly have you believe they are just Mr or Mrs Average. They are not; it is a common persuasion technique.

ALERT: Just because you are creating a site for your church does not mean these principles do not apply to you. How do you sell nutritional supplements? How do you sell religion? You sell it by framing the argument so somehow your product provides the user with happiness and fulfilment. If you practise these techniques subtly, your website will benefit by them. Every site is selling something.

? DID YOU KNOW?

The hypothetical webpage shown here is based upon the Car CSS template by Design4, and is downloaded from Open Source Web Design (www.oswd.org).

Prefer simple to complex and edit your writing

This is something I must remind myself every day. Forced sophistication is transparent and muddies writing. Instead, prefer simple words, sentences, and paragraphs to the complex. Once you have written the words, edit them. Poor grammar and spelling detract from your site's purpose, and undermine its authority. Ensure your spelling and grammar are correct.

1 Look at the My Musings webpage. Notice the forced sophistication; is it convincing?

2 Now look at the My Dilema page. The spelling and grammatical errors detract greatly from the site's content. Now if someone would believe me...

? DID YOU KNOW?

My personal recommendation is a book entitled *Edit Yourself* by Bruce Ross-Larson. His company website, www.clearwriter.com, provides online training, and links to all his books for sale on Amazon.com. This, his best book, is only around $10.

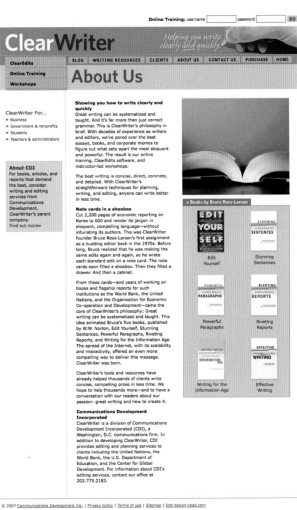

Ensure meaning is intuitive on important items

Labels, buttons, headers, hyperlinks and other important items should be labelled intuitively. The text on a hyperlink should illustrate rather than obfuscate the link's purpose. The same holds true for a button. Labelling a button Submit is best. If you must change the label, select an intuitive meaning.

1 Revisit the hypothetical webpage on page 68. Pretentious labels replace what should be clearly marked hyperlinks.

2 Now consider the labels' meanings as on the page shown here. Pretentious labels should be changed to clear hyperlinks.

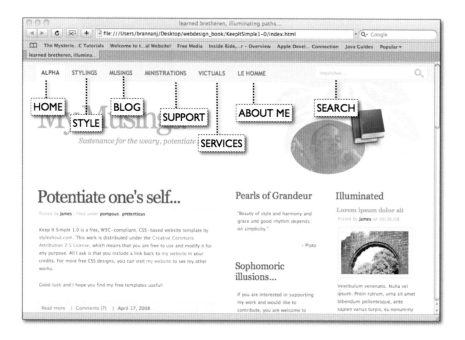

4 Webpage layout and composition

Introduction

A site might be designed well architecturally, and have thought provoking written content, but if the site's individual pages are designed poorly, the site might still fail. Successful websites do not require design on par with a graphics art magazine. You can design a much more modest site and still have the site be pleasing and successful. The key is making a page's design complement its content, helping users read and navigate through your site more easily.

Place important information above the fold line

A user's screen resolution determines a webpage's fold line. Always remember your page's fold line when developing and testing. Place important content above the fold and less important content below.

1 Navigate to www.wtopnews.com. Notice that important information is placed above the fold.

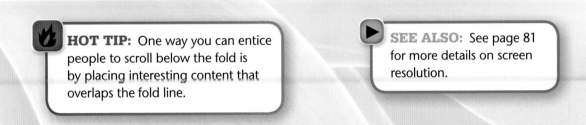

SEE ALSO: See page 81 for more details on screen resolution.

HOT TIP: One way you can entice people to scroll below the fold is by placing interesting content that overlaps the fold line.

2 Notice the hypothetical site for a motorcycle club. To ensure people scroll below the fold line, I place a woman with an exposed shoulder just above the fold line, leaving her remainder below the fold line. Nine out of 10 men will now scroll to the page's base.

Nobody reads text online, so make the page printable

I find nothing more frustrating than when I am doing online research and a site subdivides its articles into endless pages. Although chunking information is good web design, it can be maddening when reading a detailed article. Provide two article versions, one for reading online and one for printing.

1. Navigate to www.javaworld.com and find any article.

2. Scroll to the bottom and notice that to read the entire article you must navigate to several different pages. Fine if you want to read the article on your computer, but not so good if you want to read it in your bath.

3. Notice the printer icon and text link. Click the icon, and your browser reloads the article as a single page, formatted for printing.

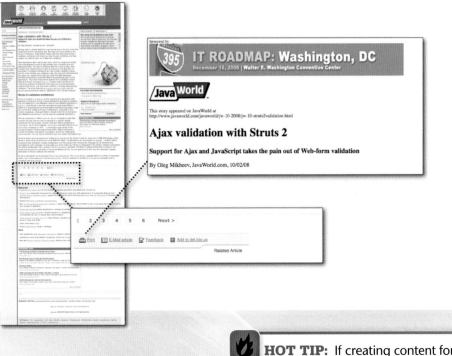

HOT TIP: If creating content for users to read, consider two versions – one version formatted for web display and the other for printing.

Use grid theory

Almost all print layouts use a grid to lay out the page. The same is true for well-designed webpages. A grid is exactly what it sounds like: it is an invisible line grid you use to position your page's elements.

1. Navigate to www.freecsstemplates.org and review the Puzzled template.

2. Notice the template uses a grid for layout.

3. Navigate to virtually any template on the site, and you will notice a distinct grid appearance.

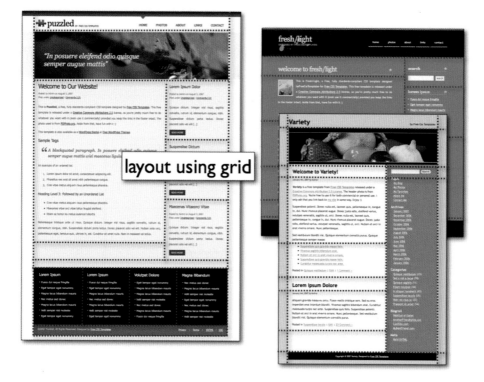

layout using grid

ALERT: Webpages are limited to horizontal and vertical grids. You cannot use CSS and HTML to create diagonal grids.

Violate a page's grid to draw attention to an element

An easy way to draw a user's attention to a certain screen area is by violating the page's natural grid. When used sparingly, violating a page's symmetry can enhance your page's design.

1 Navigate to www.rockracing.com and notice the first thing that jumps out at you is Tyler Hamilton. One reason is that his colour combination is significantly different from the page's colour scheme. Another is because he is violating the page's natural grid lines.

2 Now navigate to www.freecsstemplates.org and find the sweet garden template. Notice the page is a simple grid, except the flower, causing the flower to stand out from the page.

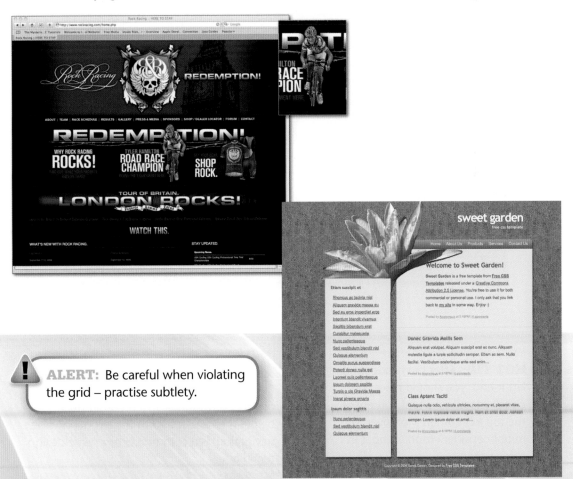

ALERT: Be careful when violating the grid – practise subtlety.

Emphasise what is important

Emphasise what is important. By emphasising what is important, users will notice the important item, and your page will be more successful.

1 Navigate to www.animenation.com. What is the first thing you notice? I bet it is the '75% overstock explosion sale'.

2 Notice how the large yellow type grabs your attention. Incidentally, notice the word 'overstock' and the figure's head slightly violate the page's natural grid, adding more emphasis.

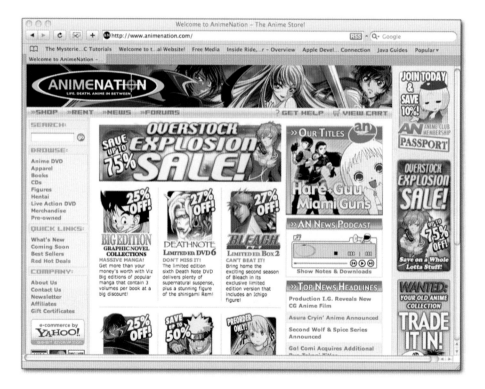

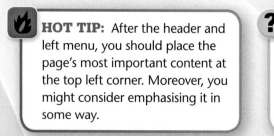

HOT TIP: After the header and left menu, you should place the page's most important content at the top left corner. Moreover, you might consider emphasising it in some way.

DID YOU KNOW?

Placing the 'big sale here' or 'buy this item' prominently in the top left corner (just below the header and to the left of any side navigation) is a common ecommerce design technique.

Prominently display your purpose, or have a tagline

If you have a clear mission, or purpose, state it on your home page. Not every page requires a mission statement. For instance, most ecommerce sites have a clear purpose. You can state your organisation's goals, your site's goals, or both if they are different.

1 Navigate to the Campaign against Euro-federalism website at www.caef.org.uk. Notice the site states the organisation's purpose directly below the banner.

2 Navigate to the Directgov website (www.direct.gov.uk) and notice it states the site's purpose in two places.

3 Navigate to the UK Department of Health's website (www.dh.gov.uk). The home page displays the department's purpose. Now click each main link and notice that each page displays its own purpose.

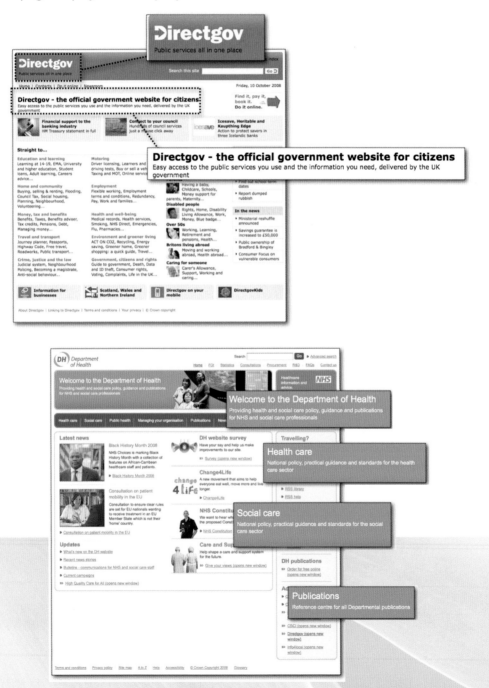

Design for a maximum screen resolution of 1024x768

Always design for a maximum screen resolution of 1024x768. Conservatively, you might consider 800x600, depending upon your target users. But realistically, these days most people's computers display at 1024x768.

1 Notice the webpage here. This site is designed for a 1900x1200 screen resolution. On a monitor with a maximum 1024x768 screen resolution, a user must scroll vertically to view the entire page's content.

1900x1200 resolution

1024x768 resolution

Photos for grandma to view on her old 640x480 Monitor

HOT TIP: Always test pages using a 1024x768 screen resolution. If conservative, use 800x600 to test.

SEE ALSO: Some users might have lower resolutions. Some web design experts still recommend 800x600. To avoid this problem entirely, refer to the 'Use a centred layout' section and see the centred, liquid layout.

2 Contrast the second example with the first. The Quartz Storage page is designed for a 1024x768 screen resolution. On monitors that can display higher resolutions, the page still looks good.

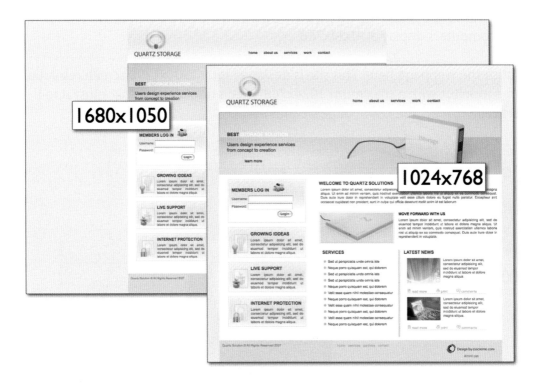

Know the difference between fixed and flexible layout

Modern webpages use cascading style sheets (CSS) to format a webpage. When a browser displays a page, it refers to the CSS page for a instructions.

HTML   CSS

Browser applies CSS stylesheet to HTML.

Displayed page in browser's viewport.

1. Refer to the Survival International page, which uses a fixed layout. As the browser's viewport shrinks, the page remains unchanged.

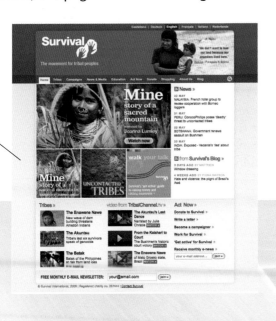

2 Now look at the Animal Health Agency's webpage, which uses a liquid layout. As the browser's viewport shrinks, the content wraps to accommodate the narrower width.

ALERT: If developing a site for a public agency, use a liquid layout. Most agencies require that you use a liquid layout because the agency wants to accommodate users with outdated browsers.

Use a centred layout

A centred layout places content centred on a larger page. The idea behind this strategy is to create a content area smaller than the page's width with gutters on both sides that expand and contract depending upon the browser's size.

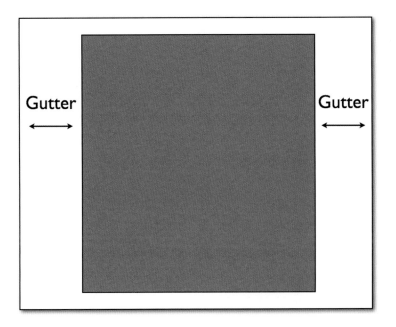

1. Refer to the hypothetical page shown in four versions on the next page. It uses a centred fixed layout. All four figures show the web browser maximised. The top page is at 1680x1050 resolution, the second is at 1024x768 resolution, the third at 800x600 and the last at 640x480. Notice the content section's width remains unchanged, although the 640x480 screen resolution does require scrolling.

2. As an aside, notice that the top page shows the background image's seam. Remember, users might have higher screen resolutions than yours, so be certain your page looks good at higher screen resolutions.

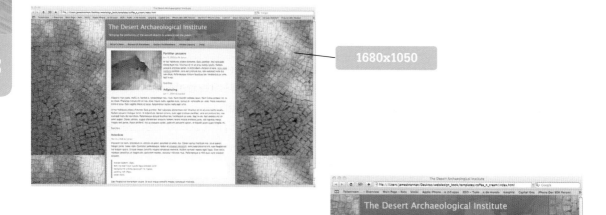

1680x1050

1024x768

800x600

640x480

3 Compare the fixed layout pages with the same pages using a centred liquid layout (see overleaf). As the screen resolution becomes smaller, the content wraps to accommodate the loss in space.

4 Finally, look at the webpage below. Notice the header repeats horizontally because the page is wider than the header image. A common strategy is using a liquid layout, with a fixed maximum width. For instance, in all the preceding webpages, the pages use a maximum width of 720 pixels, the same width as the header graphic. By stating a maximum width, I ensure the header graphic does not repeat in wider browser viewports. This webpage does not specify a maximum width and so the text widens to take most of the browser's viewport and the header's background image repeats.

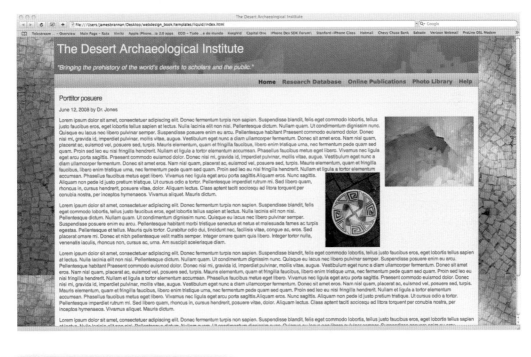

1680x1050

1024x768

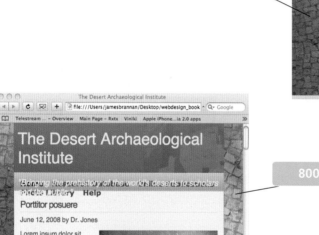

800x600

640x480

5 Using web colour effectively

Introduction

When developing a website, you usually create a colour palette containing four or five colours. You then limit the colour combinations on your pages to the colours in the palette. By consistently applying colours, your website's pages are visually appealing and consistent. Consistent sites are usable sites. Users can navigate consistent sites more quickly than haphazard ones.

Important: Most web design books begin by reviewing the colour wheel, primary colours, secondary colours, and tertiary colours. This book does not. If you want to learn colour theory, and how to create colour palettes from scratch, there are ample online resources. Instead, in this book I focus on using an available tool to make colour selections for you. I have enough trouble coordinating my wardrobe; these tools can do a much better job coordinating my webpage colours.

Have a basic understanding of RGB colour values

Computers display colours using RGB (red, green and blue). RGB displays colours additively, where 256 red shades, 256 green shades and 256 blue shades are mixed to display over 16 million colour combinations.

1 The webpage here lists several colours and each colour's RGB value as a hexadecimal number.

2 Navigate to www.google.com and search 'RGB colour values' and within seconds it presents you with more sites on RGB colour than you could ever use.

3 Navigate to one of the sites and find a colour chart. These charts are ubiquitous on the Web and are very useful.

HOT TIP: You can refer to many colours by name when using HTML and CSS.

? DID YOU KNOW?

When specifying a colour using RGB, you enter the three different red, green and blue colour amounts as percentages. When mixed, these three colour combinations form a new colour. You can use a decimal number and specify all three values separately. For instance, maroon's RGB value is 176,48,96. Black's is 0,0,0 and white's is 256,256,256. You can also specify all three values as a single hexadecimal number. For instance, maroon's hexadecimal value is 800000, black's is 000000, and white's is FFFFFF.

Use a little colour theory when designing

Rainbows are for the sky, not a webpage. Use a little colour theory when designing a webpage. Entire books devote themselves to colour theory, so this section cannot do the topic justice.

1 The hypothetical page shown here uses too many colours. A little common sense can go a long way when developing a webpage.

2 Create a palette from three or four complementary colours. Use that palette consistently. This chapter's next section discusses palettes further.

? DID YOU KNOW?

You do not really need to know much about colour theory. Many tools help you choose a consistent palette. The next section is devoted to creating a palette using a freely available online tool called Kuler.

3 You can choose the colours from a colour wheel, from experimenting or by using a tool such as Kuler. You use Kuler in this chapter's next section.

4 Search 'colour wheel' on Google, and you have many sites to select from, and at least one will have an online colour wheel you can use.

ALERT: Different cultures place different meaning on colours. For instance, in the east white is associated with mourning. In the USA and the UK, the rainbow colours are associated with lesbian, gay, bisexual and transgendered (LGBT) pride.

DID YOU KNOW?

Limiting yourself to browser safe colours was important once, now it is not. About 15 years ago, many monitors could only display 256 colours. Moreover, different browsers and operating systems displayed many identical colours differently. But there were 216 colours that both Netscape and Internet Explorer displayed the same. These 216 colours became known as the 'browser-safe' palette. Today, over 90 per cent of all web users use a 24-bit display. That means most users' browsers display 16,777,216 colours. Only 8 per cent of users are using a computer with 16-bit graphics, and even they see 65,536 colours. Less than 2 per cent of your potential users have graphic displays less than 16-bit, and I assure you, they are accustomed to a poor display.

Use a tool to generate a colour palette

What goes with the colour Hollywood Cerise? I don't have a clue but realise that I do not know, so rather than trying to determine what colours complement each other, I use a tool-generated colour palette. Tool-generated palettes are readily available online. A particularly good tool is the Adobe Air application called Kuler.

1 Navigate to kuler.adobe. com and download the Kuler Desktop.

2 Choose a swatch from Kuler, and click the hash mark to copy the colour's hexadecimal values to your computer's clipboard.

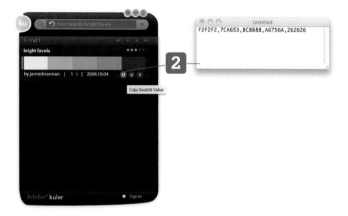

3 Open a text editor and choose paste. The hexadecimal values for each colour are pasted to the text document.

4 Create an account with Adobe on the Kuler website and log in.

5 From the left menu select Create, From an Image, and upload an image. I uploaded an image from Flickr of a Rio De Janeiro favela.

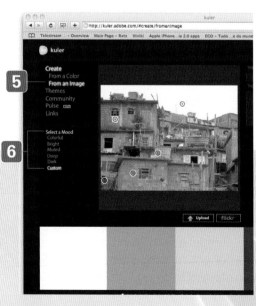

6 Notice the choices under Select a Mood. You have several choices, depending upon the mood you wish to create. Creating a page about Samba? Choose Colourful or Bright. An information site? Choose Muted. A site about gang violence and poverty's horrors? Choose Deep or Dark.

7 Save the palette, open Kuler Desktop, log in to Kuler, and the newly created palette appears.

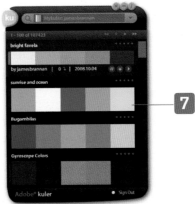

8 Review the page below that I created in about an hour using the colours determined in step 7. I modified the Discovery template by using freecsstemplates.org. I replaced the template's photos with my own, and changed the colour scheme to match my template. Easy, as Kuler and freecsstemplates.org did the hard design work for me.

? DID YOU KNOW?

The photo of the Brazilian favela is from Flickr by Nate Cull and is licensed under the Creative Commons Attribution-Share Alike 2.0 Generic licence.

Use your colour palette consistently across pages

This advice should be common sense, but surprisingly it is often not followed. Do not change your colour palette midway through your website. Every page should use the same colour palette.

1 Look at the webpages here. These two masterpieces are originals, not based upon a downloaded CSS template. I also did not use a tool like Adobe Kuler, instead relying upon my artistic sensibilities.

2 Notice the colour difference between page one and page two. The difference is as jarring as my favourite striped shirt and plaid tie I wear together when applying for web designer jobs.

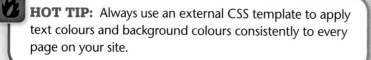

HOT TIP: Always use an external CSS template to apply text colours and background colours consistently to every page on your site.

Choose colours to match your site's mood

This is another topic that should be common sense, yet it is important enough to state as a separate best practice. Your colour choice should reflect the mood you wish to convey. A tool like Kuler Desktop makes selecting a colour palette to reflect a certain mood much easier.

1 Suppose you wanted to create a sombre, dark site devoted to horror films. What colours should you choose?

2 Start Adobe Kuler and enter death into the search bar, and then review the colours. The swatch, entitled appropriately enough death, looks promising.

3 Enter horror into the search bar and review the colours returned. The swatch entitled gothic seems a good choice.

4 Now search for circus, and Kuler returns bright, cheerful colours. Search for office, and Kuler returns colours found in most offices.

ALERT: You can always modify a chosen template or use a photograph to generate a colour combination. For instance, if I selected the death palette, I would probably replace a grey colour with a deep, blood-red. If I wanted to use a photo, I would find one of a graveyard, or something equally spooky, and use it to generate my palette.

Accept that colour choices may not appear as you wish

Some systems and monitors are better than others. You must accept this fact and realise that your artistic creations might not always appear to your exact specification.

1 Navigate to the Name that Colour website (www.chir.org/phernalia/name-that-colour) and notice the sunset graphic. It uses subtle colour shading to great effect; it is just a slightly less great effect than that displayed on my Daewoo.

2 Here you can see my MacBook laptop's screen. The other image has been modified to resemble the graphic's appearance on my surplus Daewoo monitor that I got for free on CraigsList (www.craigslist.org).

3 On the Daewoo, the colours aren't as brilliant, the subtle shading is slightly less subtle, and the colours are slightly washed-out.

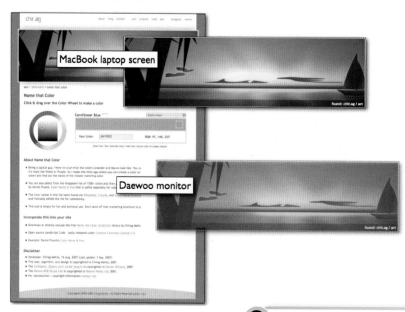

MacBook laptop screen

Daewoo monitor

? DID YOU KNOW?

Monitors sometimes render colours incorrectly, and all your hard work getting an exact shade might be wasted effort. Before you design that perfect graphic, using colours such as Akaroa, Citrine White or Seashell Peach, realise that what you produce might be slightly off, depending upon a user's monitor.

? DID YOU KNOW?

As I write this book on my MacBook, my second display is a surplus Daewoo monitor. The monitor, compared to my brand new Apple MacBook's display, doesn't show colours not as brightly and adds a subtle grey tint.

Use text and background colour harmoniously

Make text and background colours work harmoniously together. Better yet, keep your background white or off white (I prefer whitesmoke) and your text black. Ensuring your colours have sufficient contrast keeps your site readable.

1 The first image shown here is a light gray background with dimgray text. Legible, but not optimal if the site is a text-heavy information site that readers go to for information.

2 The second image is a whitesmoke background with dimgray text. It is slightly easier to read, and would probably be sufficient for most readers.

3 The third image is a whitesmoke background with black text. It's easy to read, but does not match the site's colours or style. Although all three are suitable choices, my choice would be whitesmoke with a dimgray text for this site.

ALERT: Remember your audience. If you were developing a site for senior citizens, you might strongly consider a white background with black text. People's ability to distinguish light shade differences tends to diminish with age.

? DID YOU KNOW?

Colours must have sufficient contrast between the background and text. Insufficient contrast makes your site unusable to some people, particularly those with disabilities. A good rule is that if your site's text is illegible when viewed on a black and white monitor, you should change your background and foreground colour combination.

6 Texture

Introduction

As I have demonstrated in my hypothetical webpages, I am not an artist. My sensibilities lie more towards information architecture and development. I will not even try explaining texture. Instead, let me quote from a graphic design book.

As Ellen Lupton and Jennifer Cole Phillips stated in *Graphic Design, The New Basics*: '*Texture is the tactile grain of surfaces and substances. Textures in our environment help us understand the nature of things; rose bushes have sharp thorns to protect the delicate flowers they surround; smooth, paved roads signal safe passage; thick fog casts a veil on our view*'.

Important: This chapter is potentially damaging. When I get creative with texture, perspective, and light, the result is usually a design nightmare (see below). When in doubt, leave it out.

Consider adding subtle texture to your background

Texture, in the wrong hands, can kill a website. But sometimes you might wish to convey a certain mood or feeling using a texture. Usually, you achieve texture using something called wallpaper. Wallpaper is an image, usually of a texture such as burlap, that repeats across a page's background, giving the illusion of a continuous texture on the page's surface.

1 Note the background patterns shown here. A background pattern is usually a small swatch that can repeat seamlessly on a page, providing the illusion of a continuous image.

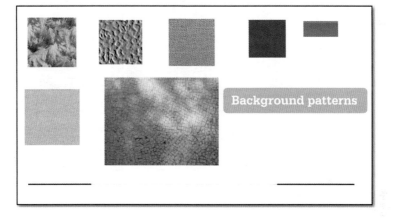

Background patterns

2 Navigate to Rock Racing's website (www.rockracing.com). Most high-end racing bikes and parts are constructed of black carbon fibre, and so Rock Racing chose a carbon fibre background textured wallpaper.

3 Note the banner graphic's carbon fibre texture.

4 Scroll to the page's base and notice the carbon fibre background is again visible.

5 Notice also that the graphics have a faint carbon fibre background.

6 Finally, notice that the bulk of the page is plain black. There is no background texture to interfere with readability.

Consider starting from an Adobe Photoshop template

CSS allows you to specify background images on entire pages and individual elements such as <div> elements. A common technique is to create a graphic mock-up of the page's background using Adobe Photoshop, cut the template into smaller graphics, and then place the cut images as background images in the actual CSS template.

1 The template here illustrates this technique. The CSS template designer, Dieter Schneider, originally created an Adobe Photoshop document. He then cut the document into numerous images, and used the images as the CSS templates' background.

2 Download the template and open it in your web browser. It appears as a single image. Open the page's CSS style sheet in a text editor and note that the CSS combines the images into the original Photoshop image.

3 Search for 'tutorial web template CSS photoshop' on Google. It presents you with many tutorials explaining this techniques' particulars.

? **DID YOU KNOW?**

You can download and use the free CSS template, Lonelyness, at Open Source Web Design (www.oswd.org).

Use perspective to add depth and direct the eye

Perspective is another design technique, which when used incorrectly can result in a design nightmare. Used subtly, it can help your design guide the user through your content.

1 Download the Outside CSS template by styleshout.com. Notice the template follows good usability best practices by placing the logo on the upper left corner.

2 But notice the photograph. It directs your eye away from the logo. A photograph usually draws a viewer's eye towards its centre. The eye then follows any strong lines in the photograph. The fence line in the photograph draws the eye away from the logo. The beach and sea intersection does draw the eye towards the logo, but the fence's pull overshadows the beach and sea intersection.

3 Notice the same template with the photo reversed. It draws the viewer's eye towards the logo.

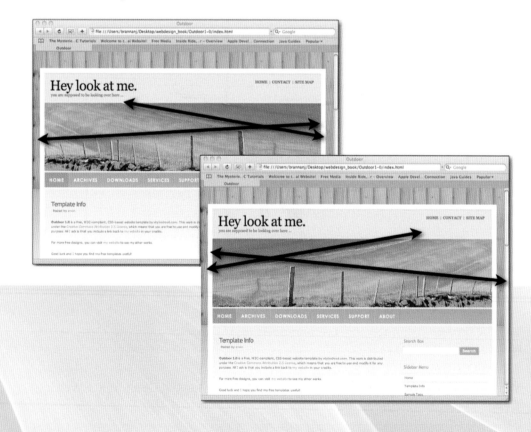

Use drop-shadows and light to create perspective and depth

Adding drop-shadow and light to your images helps create perspective and depth. This has an especially dramatic effect when combined with violating a page's symmetry. Of course, as with other design techniques, you should use this technique sparingly.

1 Look at the cyclist Tyler Hamilton on Rock Racing's website shown on page 104. This is an example of effectively using drop-shadow subtlety.

2 Look at page 93. Although less subtle than the Rock Racing example, it is also a good design using drop-shadows.

3 Now compare those two examples with mine. Practise subtlety, and almost any design technique works.

HOT TIP: Use drop-shadows and items with transparent backgrounds that float on a page sparingly. If you do not, you might end up with a page resembling the James A. Brannan original shown here.

ALERT: Currently, drop-shadows are unstylish while reflections are in vogue. However, reflections might be passé tomorrow. So use reflections with restraint. Slight drop-shadows help text stand out from a background or give the illusion that an image floats above the page.

Remember, fads come and go: when in doubt, use a grid

My design skills are challenged. Left to my own devices, I would use drop-shadows, reflections, textured backgrounds, and every weapon in my design arsenal to trick you into thinking my page was three-dimensional. Problem is, the page is two-dimensional. Remember, what users really want is pleasing, easy to find content that they can easily digest.

1. Using a grid does not imply your site must be boring. Look at the page for the United States Navy, which although very stylish and sophisticated, uses a simple grid layout. It even uses an interesting animation.

2. Consider the Navy's .mil website. This site packs considerable information onto one page, and the page's design is still appealing and professional.

3. Finally, consider the Flash website template. Although visually striking, it is not usable if your site presents substantive information.

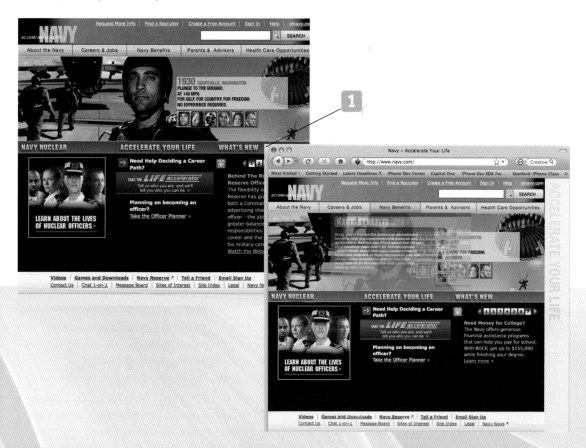

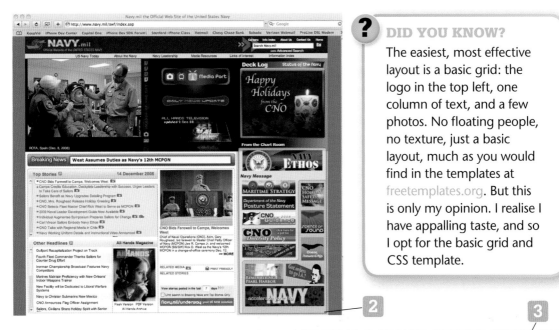

2

3

? **DID YOU KNOW?**

The easiest, most effective layout is a basic grid: the logo in the top left, one column of text, and a few photos. No floating people, no texture, just a basic layout, much as you would find in the templates at freetemplates.org. But this is only my opinion. I realise I have appalling taste, and so I opt for the basic grid and CSS template.

? **DID YOU KNOW?**

The Flash template is a free template at FlashVillage.com. Being fair to the template designer, the Flash template was probably not designed for an informative website, but rather a personal website, like a fiction author's site, for instance. Suppose you were a crime novelist, the template shown here would be very appropriate. Again, almost all design rules can be broken depending upon circumstance.

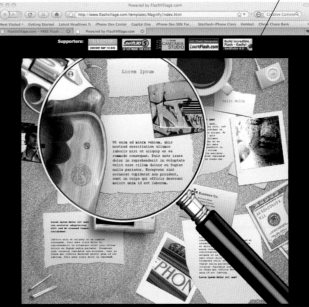

! **ALERT:** Being trendy ensures your site ages quickly. Instead, aim for usability, consistency and a clean design. It really is not important if you use drop-shadows or reflections. Either work when used in moderation. Now if I can just remember moderation the next time I want to add to my website a cool tattoo graphic of a scantily clad model holding a flaming skull wrapped in barbed wire.

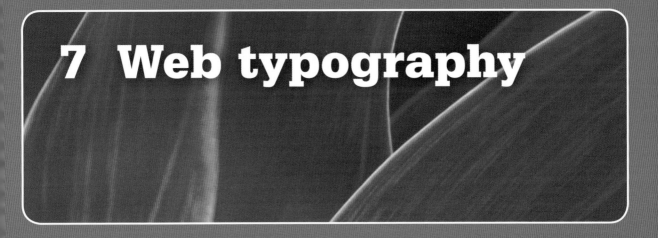

7 Web typography

Introduction

Wikipedia defines typography as 'the art and technique of arranging type, type design, and modifying type glyphs'. Typography is choosing fonts and formatting text on a page so the page is visually pleasing to readers. Creating a webpage does not require an advanced proficiency with typography, but you should have a basic understanding of typography. This chapter provides just that, by presenting several best practices. Following these best practices will make your content easier to read and more visually appealing.

Understand fonts

A font is a design for letters, numbers and other characters. It is a pitch, size and typeface combination. A typeface is a font-family, for instance Arial is a typeface. Although technically incorrect, a typeface is not a font, but in web vernacular, the two are the same.

1. Here we show several Arial fonts. Arial Bold 12pt is a font, Arial is a typeface.

2. Typefaces are divided into two major categories, serif and sans serif. Serif fonts add little serifs at letter ends while sans serif fonts do not.

3. You can also divide typefaces depending upon whether they are monospaced or proportional. Proportional fonts are easier to read and are what you would typically use on your site. Monospace fonts are usually reserved for mathematical formulae, computer code, and similar special text.

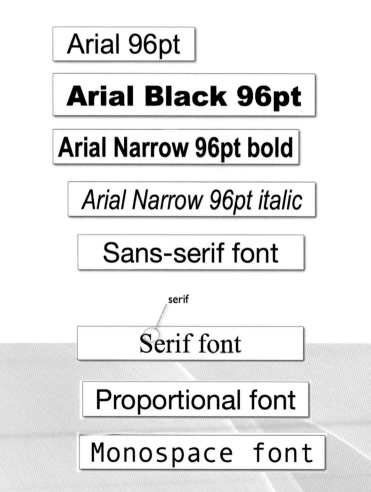

Only use browser-safe fonts and give a font option

When a browser downloads a webpage, the user's operating system limits the fonts available to the browser. Browsers use a computer's fonts. If the font specified by the page's CSS code is not available, the browser cannot display the text using the specified font and instead uses its default font, as shown in this example.

1 Suppose I decided to be creative and changed the header fonts to the Baskerville font in the hypothetical page here.

2 Because I have Baskerville installed on my Apple MacBook, Safari renders the font correctly.

3 When I use Firefox on Windows XP to display the page, I do not have the font installed, and so it defaults to the browser's default font, which I had set to Courier.

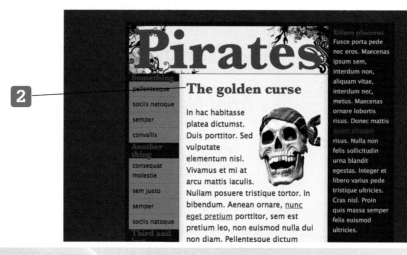

4 When I modify the CSS to use an alternative font or a font-family, as shown below, Safari displays the Baskerville font and Firefox on Windows displays using the alternative font, Arial.

`h1 {color: firebrick; font-family: Baskerville,Arial}`

alternative font

Try not to specify a font size unless it is a relative size

Reading text on a monitor is difficult; do not make it more difficult by using small fonts. Even better, do not specify a font size. Instead, use a relative measurement, such as em or a percentage. Here FireFox allows setting the default font using the Preferences dialogue.

1 The hypothetical webpage here specifies its font as 12pt. When I change my browser's default font to Times 24pt, the page's fonts remain unchanged. Using a font size allows precise layout; however, it ignores a user's preferences. Ignoring a user's preferences is a bad thing; let the user specify his or her desired font size.

2 Now consider the second webpage, which specifies its font as 1.2 em. Now when I change my browser's default font to Times 20pt, the page's font size changes to reflect my preferred font size, as 1.2 em is relative to my preferred font size.

ALERT: Resist the urge to control your page's font size. It is rude; it says to users 'I don't care about your preferences'.

HOT TIP: Currently, it is trendy to specify small fonts. Many web designers adhering to the so-called Web 2.0 design fad specify text sizes smaller than the user's default font size. Resist this trend. If a user specifies his or her font as something outlandishly large, for instance. Courier 24pt, it is your job to ensure your page displays well in the user's browser. Do not take the easy, but user unfriendly, shortcut and make the font smaller. Remember, the user might have a disability and cannot read small fonts. I am very nearsighted, for instance, and I have difficulty reading fonts under 14pt on a computer screen. Do not make me squint to read your site – respect your users.

ALERT: Using a relative measure such as em or a percentage makes your webpage more accessible to users. Sight-impaired users can set their browser font large, and your site's fonts are displayed relative to the larger size.

Make your text legible by using enough leading

Most people find reading single-spaced manuscripts difficult. Distinguishing between single-spaced sentences causes eyestrain. Now compound the inherent difficulties of reading text on a computer screen with the difficulties of reading single-spaced text, and the result is text which is virtually impossible to read.

1 Notice on the webpage here the single-spaced excerpt and how difficult it is to read the page.

2 Now refer to the double-spaced excerpt; the page is much easier to read when double-spaced.

? DID YOU KNOW?

Leading is a typographer's term for line spacing. You can control leading with CSS. You should specify a leading that is 1.5 spacing to 2 spacing (single and a half spaced or double spaced). Wider leading is appropriate in some special circumstances, but 1.5 to 2 spacing is usually the most appropriate line spacing. For more information on setting spacing using CSS, refer to a CSS book.

Left align text and headings

We read from left to right in the western world. Right justifying or centring large text blocks makes reading a page's text harder. When text is right or centre justified, a user must search for a line's beginning, tiring the user's eyes more quickly. Left justifying text makes reading the text easier, as the user's eyes do not search for a line's beginning.

1 Consider the hypothetical page here, which is right justified. Notice how the ragged left edges force your eyes to scan to find each line's beginning.

2 The second page is justified. Justifying text means that both left and right margins are aligned straight. Print media use this technique, but justified text is a poor choice for web text. Using print media, typesetters can exercise fine control over a paragraph's layout. For instance, typesetters of a printed page can manually modify a page and add hyphens as needed. The Web does not allow this fine control over word spacing and so justified text often appears awkward.

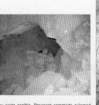

ALERT: Personally I find the expert's advice subjective when discussing left aligned compared to justified. In this section's example, I think both left and justified look fine.

3 The third page centres its text. Centring text is an obviously poor choice, as now both left and right edges are ragged.

4 The fourth page left justifies its text. The lines are easy to read, and it appears natural.

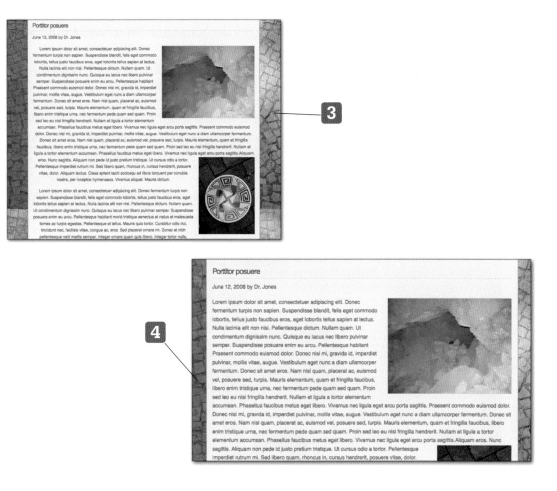

HOT TIP: When a paragraph has a heading, if the paragraph is not justified, do not centre the heading. Only centre the heading when its associated paragraph's text is justified.

Never underline text

This best practice should seem intuitive. Hyperlinks are underlined. If you underline words other than hyperlinks, you confuse your site's users.

1 Consider the hypothetical corporate site shown here. It is based upon the CSS template, Collaboration, by freecsstemplates.org.

2 The introductory paragraph on espionage underlines text to emphasise the text. The only difference between emphasised text and hyperlinks is that the hyperlinks are slightly darker.

3 Now notice the second version, where the emphasised text is either emboldened or italicised. The text is still formatted poorly, but users can clearly distinguish between emphasised text and hyperlinks.

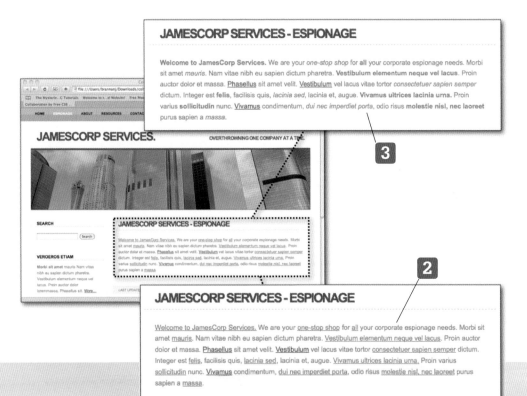

Consider not using capital letters

Using too many capital letters reduces text legibility. Never capitalise an entire word to emphasise the word, instead embolden or enlarge the word. Also, avoid initial capitalising headings. Unless a formal noun, capitalise only a heading's first letter.

1 Notice the first page shown here. This page capitalises its headings.

2 The second page initial capitalises its headings.

3 The third page's headings capitalise only the first letter of the first word.

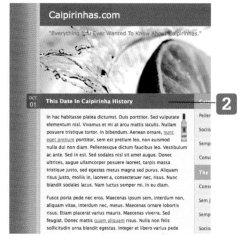

ALERT: I find the experts' advice subjective in this section. Personally, I think all three styles look fine in the example webpages in this section.

? DID YOU KNOW?
I based the hypothetical webpage used in this section on the Bitter Sweet CSS template by Arcsin.

Place links as you would footnotes

Rather than interspersing your text with hyperlinks, try placing the links at your content's bottom, similar to footnotes. Be sparing when including links in your text, as hyperlinks reduce text legibility. The hyperlink looks different to its surrounding text. This difference forces a user's eye to slow down when scanning the text. The hyperlink is also distracting, as a user sees it is a hyperlink.

1 Review the hypothetical webpage here. It has hyperlinks scattered throughout the text.

2 Now review the same page, with significantly fewer scattered hyperlinks. It has only a couple of text hyperlinks and includes the remainder below the content under a 'Further Reading' header, which makes it much more readable.

? **DID YOU KNOW?**

I based the webpage in this section upon the Bee CSS template by Minimalistic Design, www.minimalistic-design.net.

8 Images

Introduction

Imagining a magazine, or webpage, without images is difficult. Images convey important information and add an entertaining aspect to webpages. In this chapter, you will explore several best practices for including images on your site. The chapter's purpose is to familiarise you enough with web graphics so you can effectively add them to your website, and have the graphics be relevant and visually pleasing.

Important: Manipulating images has a large opportunity cost. Unless you are adept at using graphic editing tools, obtaining the 'just-right' look can consume your time budget. Consider hiring a graphics designer.

Use JPEG for photographs and PNG for everything else

Use the Joint Photographers Expert Group (JPEG) format for photographs and the Portable Network Graphics (PNG) format for everything else. Unless creating an animated Graphics Interchange Format (GIF), forget about GIFs. GIFs are outdated.

1 Notice the GIF's halo on the webpage of ants. When using a GIF, if you wish your graphics to be 'antialised', you must select a transparent colour similar to your site's background colour. If you do not, you obtain a 'halo' effect. PNG uses alpha channels for its transparency, allowing variable transparency, meaning no 'halos'.

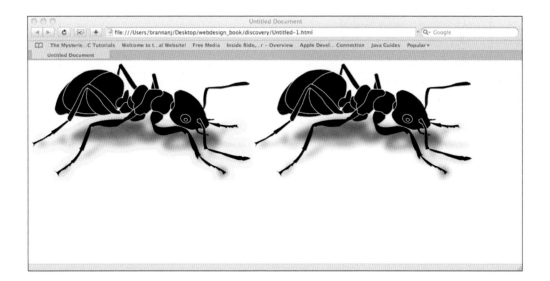

 DID YOU KNOW?

The PNG format replaces the older GIF format. The PNG format's origins date to 1995, and were a response to the company Unisys obtaining a patent for the computer algorithm used in the GIF format. The PNG has no patents and is free.

2 Now look at the second webpage. When using a drop-shadow in a GIF, the page's background must match the GIF's transparent background. PNGs do not have this requirement.

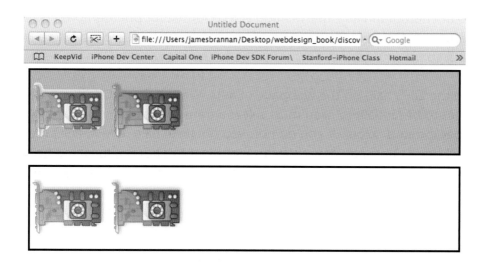

? DID YOU KNOW?
GIF files use the .gif extension, PNG uses the .png extension, and JPEG uses the .jpg extension. A JPEG file might also use the less common .jpeg extension.

! ALERT: Internet Explorer 6 and earlier do not support PNG adaptive transparency, but do support PNG index transparency.

! ALERT: PNG does not support animation like GIFs do; if you wish to have an animation you must choose GIF. However, Flash does a much better job with animation, so this advantage of a GIF is tenuous. You should use Flash to create animations.

Don't steal graphics and be wary of 'free' graphics

Do not steal images from another website. It is an easy invitation for others to sue you for copyright violation. If you simply must have an image, email the site's owner and find out the image's source. Try to get permission legally. Free or low-cost image sources on the Web are ubiquitous; there is no reason to steal.

Beware of 'free', though. 'Free' is a nebulous term on the Web. Free could mean you have permission to use an image personally, but, if you use the image in a public forum, then you must pay. Free could also mean free for individual use, but not for an organisation. Free could mean that the site's owner gathered images from various sites and decided to offer these images to others. He or she may, or may not, know the licensing terms of the images offered. Free is meaningless. Instead, refer to the copyright and the licence.

1. Navigate to www.google.com and search for 'Flickr sued Virgin Mobile' and then navigate to one of the sites returned. In 2007 a family sued Virgin Mobile for using an image of their teenage daughter without their permission. The photo was licensed under the Creative Commons Licence, but the family never signed a model release.

2. Now search for 'copyright infringement lawsuit web' and Google returns many articles on copyright infringement related to web matters.

3. Finally, perform another Google search, only this time search for 'free web graphics'. Navigate to a few of the sites.

4. Navigate to www.free-graphics.com. Navigate to the clipart and scroll to the page's bottom. There you will find the disclaimer, which I quote below.

   Disclaimer: Here you will find clip art collected from various websites, contributors and binary newsgroups. To the best of our knowledge, all of the clip art images available here are in the public domain and can be freely used by anyone. If you have evidence suggesting that one or more of the images existing on this server is copyrighted, then please e-mail us the details and we will remove them immediately.

You should not use this site's graphics, as you do not know the licensing. Moreover, the disclaimer makes it clear the site's author doesn't know the image licences either.

5 Now navigate to www.gnome-look.org. Select any wallpaper, icon or other media. Notice the licensing terms are clearly marked. For instance the 'an eye' wallpaper is GPL, or the GNU General Public Licence, and so you cannot use this on your website unless you wish to make your site GPL.

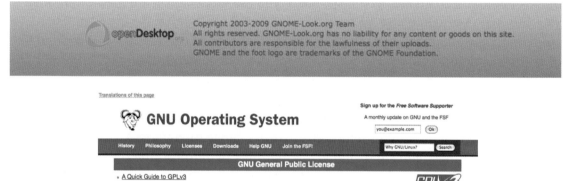

Don't steal by hot-linking

Hot-linking is stealing another site's images or multimedia content by directly linking to the content from your own site. Images and video on your HTML page are links to the binary content. As a browser processes an HTML page, as it reaches an HTML image element, the browser fetches the image from the specified location. Usually the location is on the same site as the page, in your images folder, for instance. But the location does not have to be in your images folder, the URL can point to any resource on the Web. Pointing to an external site's images is called hot-linking.

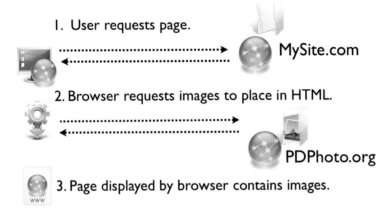

1. User requests page. MySite.com

2. Browser requests images to place in HTML.

PDPhoto.org

3. Page displayed by browser contains images.

1 Look at James's Web Site. As a page loads, it replaces an HTML tag with the actual image. The HTML tag tells a browser where to get the image. When using a properly licensed image, the image should be on your own site, where you pay your website hosting company for the space and bandwidth.

2 The page shown is particularly bad, as not only am I hot-linking to graphics, I'm stealing the bandwidth from a site that provides open source images, such as PDPhoto.org.

ALERT: If hot-linking seems like a good idea to you, realise that you could get caught. There are tools for detecting hot-linking, and hot-linking is copyright violation.

```
<html>
<body>
<h1>James's Web Site (Hot-Linking)</h1>
<img src="http://www.pdphoto.org/jons/pictures5/balboa_10_20040829_bg.jpg" width="500" height="400"/>
<img src="http://www.pdphoto.org/jons/pictures/beltaine_20_bg_050402.jpg" widht="500" height="300"/>
</body>
</html>
```

? DID YOU KNOW?

Hot-linking is similar to stealing electricity; you get the benefits without incurring costs. Web hosts charge clients based on bandwidth used; if you hot-link to another image, the other site incurs the bandwidth charge.

Use images licensed under the Creative Commons licence

You can use images licensed under the Creative Commons licence. The Creative Commons licensing terms can be confusing at first, but understanding them is important if you want to use images from Flickr.

1 Look at Table 8.1 that summarises the Creative Commons licensing schemes. Below is the licence appearance and if you go to http://creativecommons.org/about/licenses, you will see the icons that usually appear on CC licensed images.

Table 8.1 The Creative Commons licensing schemes

Scheme	What it means
Attribution	You can use the work and derive works from the work, but you must give credit to the original creator.
Noncommercial	You can only use the work noncommercially.
No Derivative Works	You can only use the original work and cannot derive new works from the original.
Share Alike	You must license your derivative work under the same licence as the original.

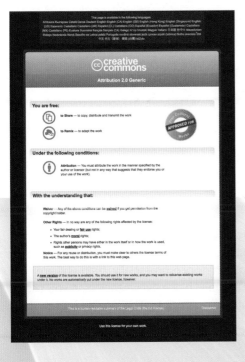

HOT TIP: If you want to use photographs with people, go to one of the many royalty-free photograph sites, where the subjects are paid models. Usually the photos are only a few pounds each.

2 Navigate to www.flickr.com. Enter monkey in the search box and click search. After the results appear, click on the Advanced Search link next to the search button.

3 Scroll down the advanced search form until you reach the Creative Commons tickboxes. Tick all three boxes. This limits your search to images you may use commercially and may modify.

4 Click Search and Flickr returns over 7000 matches. More monkeys than you could ever use on your site.

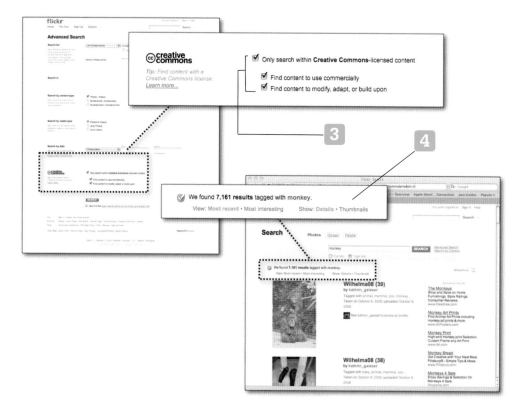

ALERT: A CC licensed photograph does not constitute a person's consent to be photographed. The Creative Commons licence applies only to copyright. If the photograph is in a public location, and you are using the photograph noncommercially, then you are probably fine, as a person cannot expect privacy in a public place. Nevertheless, if you use the photo commercially, you might be violating that person's rights. The legality is grey, and I am no lawyer, so be very careful.

Avoid clipart, use icons instead

If you want to convey an amateurish impression, nothing works better than clipart and animated GIFS. Clipart is small, cartoonish images included with many popular presentation applications such as Microsoft PowerPoint. Although convenient, they almost never convey a professional appearance. Do not use them. Use icons instead, but if you use icons, use high-quality, free icons.

1 Review the sample of icons from Crystal Project. Notice the icons' consistent and professional appearance. I obtained these icons from the www.kde-look.org website. You can also obtain them from the creator's website: www.everaldo.com. The icons are licensed LGPL.

? DID YOU KNOW?

The kde-look.org website is part of opendesktop.org. A sister website is gnome-look.org, where you can also find high-quality icons, such as the icon set Oxygen Refit 2.

! ALERT: Although unclear legally (to me at least), the GPL may require you to make your website's source code GPL if you use an icon set.

2 Navigate to www.kde-look.org and find the search form at the bottom of the ARTWORK menu on the page's left. Without entering anything, click Search.

3 Click on the licence drop-down; notice you can limit your results by a work's licence. Search for Crystal Project, and you will find the icon theme. Most results on www.kde-look.org are much more professional than any clipart you will find on a 'free clipart' site.

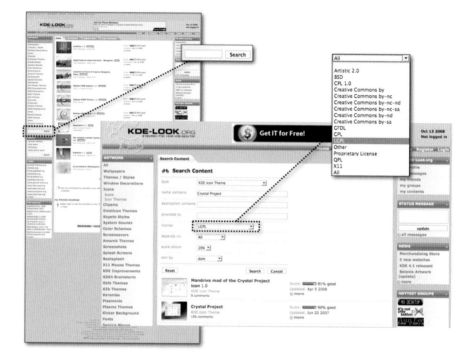

ALERT: If using KDE-LOOK to find icons or clipart, ensure the particular collection's licence is LGPL, or Creative Commons – Attribution. Alternatively, contact the creator to license the work.

HOT TIP: If choosing an icon collection, try using icons from the same collection. This helps your page maintain a consistent appearance.

ALERT: Do not use banner ad animation as a role model for including animated GIFS. Banner ads have one purpose: capturing your attention. The only thing an advertiser cares about is that you see his or her ad. So animated women dance next to promises to lower your mortgage interest rate, and cute jumping puppies sell web-hosting services. But the puppies and dancing girls are there solely to get your attention, not to make your browsing more aesthetic. Leave this nonsense to advertisers.

Use the alt attribute for images on your webpage

HTML documents include images using the <img> tag. Image tags have an attribute called alt, short for alternative, which provides alternative text if the image cannot be displayed. Ensure all images have an alt tag.

Here we can see Firefox displaying a page without graphics enabled.

HOT TIP: Blind users rely upon screen readers for browsing websites. Screen readers read an image's alt attribute to the user. If you have no alt attribute, the blind user cannot access the image's content. If your site needs to be accessible to the blind, always use the alt attribute for every image.

Format your image before using it on a webpage

Digital cameras are great. You point, you click, you upload, and you send. Problem is these files are usually huge. Many modern email providers help you avoid sending Auntie a large file by asking if you wish to reduce the image's dimensions, and size, prior to sending. You should do the same before using an image on your website.

1 Notice that the second photo's dimensions are huge. Reduce the image's dimensions if you want to use it on a webpage.

2 As I use a Macintosh, I simply use Preview to edit the photo. Any image editing software provides the same functionality.

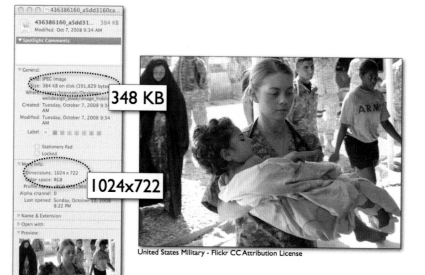

United States Military - Flickr CC Attribution License

ALERT: Images have a dimension. This is the image's length and width. Images have a size. This is the image's file size on disk. Here the photo's file size is 384 KB and its dimensions are 1024x722 pixels.

? DID YOU KNOW?

PNG is also appropriate for photographs, but JPEG usually creates a much smaller file size. For now, JPEG remains the preferred format for displaying photographs on the Web.

3 First, determine the banner image's dimensions. The image's width is 1280 pixels and its height is 856 pixels.

4 Reduce your picture's size. Select Tools, Adjust Size, and change the image's dimensions to 400x267. Preview reduces the image's size on disk from 153.4 KB to 32 KB.

? DID YOU KNOW?

The JPEG format is the standard format for displaying photographs. Use it. JPEG allows true colour. JPEG also has a compression scheme that allows the image's size to be optimised. Moreover, JPEG compression level is variable so you can choose from no compression to maximum compression when saving the image in a graphics editor. Maximum compression creates the lowest quality images while no compression creates the highest quality images. Maximum compression creates a small file size, but an ugly image. No compression creates a high-quality image, but a large file size. Medium compression is a compromise between file size and appearance, and is usually the best choice for web graphics.

4

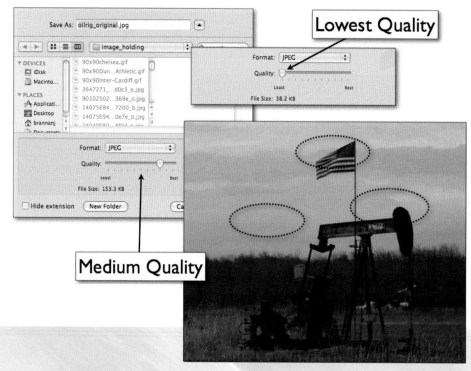

Lowest Quality

Medium Quality

Before adding the image, ask yourself if it is relevant

This best practice is common sense, but commonly not followed. Before adding an image, ask yourself if the image is relevant to the page. If it is not relevant, do not include it. If choosing images for your header template, choose images relevant to the entire site. If choosing images for content, choose images relevant to the content.

1 Look at the Survival International webpage. The photographs directly relate to the issues discussed. There is no stock photography. Including a picture of another tribe on a news article about the Enawene Nawe's dire predicament would be inappropriate.

2 Now look at the webpage on page 93. This website advertises phone directories for the gay and lesbian community. There are no required photographs for the site and so stock photos are appropriate.

3 Now refer to the hypothetical webpage overleaf about how I train for bicycle races. Be careful when adding images to your site. A user could easily mistake decorative photography for photographs of you or your organisation. The image is not of me, but the page certainly makes the image appear to be. This might be an extreme example, but you get the idea. Ask yourself if the image might create any false impressions.

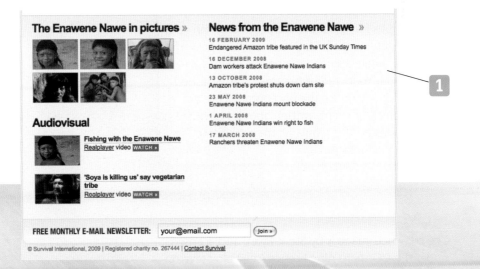

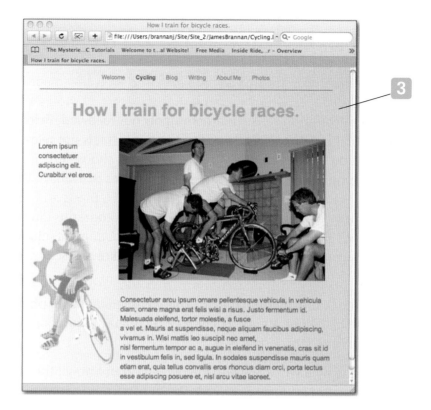

3

❓ DID YOU KNOW?

The bike race image is by Steve Ryan, and licensed under the CC Share-Alike licence (see Velo Steve on Flickr.com). The photo is for illustrative purposes only and does not imply his consent.

Crop your image

Professional photographers crop images before considering the image complete. Usually images contain detail not relevant to the photo's subject. You should crop images to remove unnecessary detail. Cropping creates a photo with a more precise message. Cropping also reduces a photo's dimensions, which results in a smaller file size. Smaller file sizes result in faster download times.

1 Notice the oil derrick in the first image. It is 1280x856 pixels and 153 K, much too large for a regular webpage with content. Reducing the dimensions to 400x267 pixels (as in the second image) reduces the file size, but notice the oil rig's detail is lost. Instead crop the image, and then reduce its dimensions.

2 After cropping, reduce the image's size to 269x300. Cropping the image before reducing its dimensions results in a 28 K file size, and the image captures more of the oil rig's detail.

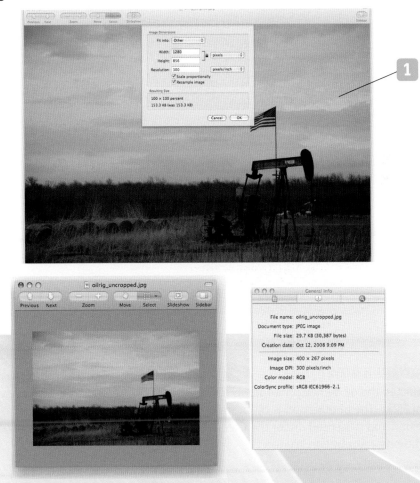

HOT TIP: Before cropping, and reducing the image's size, back up the original image.

Consider using thumbnails if appropriate

If your site displays a considerable number of photographs, or needs a detailed graphic to illustrate a concept, consider using thumbnails. A thumbnail is a smaller, lower quality image displayed instead of the original. A hyperlink is added to the thumbnail so that when clicked, the original is displayed. By providing a thumbnail, you do not needlessly consume bandwidth with photographs a user might not want to view.

1 Consider this hypothetical webpage, which is a simple photograph album page created using Apple's iWeb. The page displays thumbnails of the photographs I added. By displaying the thumbnails, a user's browser must only load the thumbnails.

2 Upon clicking the photograph, the page replaces the thumbnail with the larger, more detailed photograph.

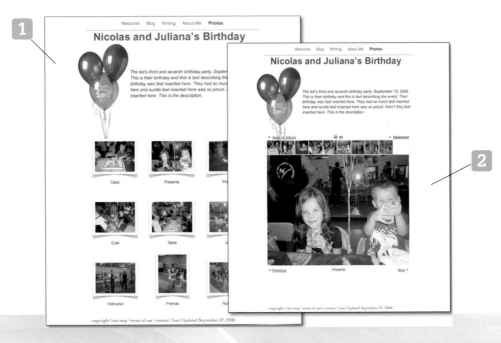

ALERT: Note, do not use hot-linking when using thumbnails. Creating a thumbnail of an image and placing the thumbnail on your website, but linking to the original larger image on someone else's site, is bandwidth theft and probably copyright violation.

9 Using multimedia effectively

Introduction

Multimedia should enhance a site's message. You can create dramatic effects and interesting online multimedia presentations. Search Google for a recent big-budget Hollywood movie. Find the movie's official site; chances are it is an impressive multimedia experience. In this chapter, I discuss several simple ways to include multimedia on your site. If you are looking for advice on creating an interactive, multimedia website, you will be disappointed. Instead, I discuss several options you might provide to a user if he or she wishes to view or listen to multimedia content. You might think I am a curmudgeon in this chapter, but remember, your site should provide a service. Choking a user's browser with needless Flash animation, background music and auto-playing video detracts from your site's service. However, using multimedia judiciously can enhance your site's service.

Do not play background music

Did you know you could embed background music in a page? The easiest way to add music is by using the HTML embed element or object element. However, do not do it. Embedding music, and then having your page automatically play the music when a user loads the page, is annoying. Moreover, users might not share your musical tastes.

1 Find the most annoying song in your CD collection. Play it a couple of times, so it is stuck in your head.

2 Hum the song for the next three or four sections in this chapter. Note how annoying it is.

3 Alternatively, go to your local public library, maximise your laptop's volume and then navigate to a website with embedded audio.

4 Suppose, despite this section's advice, you still decide to include background music. Then be certain you allow the user to turn off the music if he or she wishes.

> 🔥 **HOT TIP:** Do not automatically play any multimedia content, be it Flash animation, video or audio. Let the user select if he or she wishes to experience the content.

Avoid Flash splash screens

Yes, it is true, cool splash screens are not cool but rather, an annoyance. By providing a Flash splash screen you are sending users a clear message: form is more important than content. In some situations, this might be true. For instance, maybe it is a movie site or some multimedia studio. But I would argue that even these sites might consider avoiding a splash screen.

1 Look at the Flash splash animation here.

2 Notice the option to skip the splash screen in the lower right corner. If you simply must have a cool splash screen, provide an option for users who do not have Flash, or do not wish to experience your brilliance. Provide a link just below the animation to skip the splash screen.

Consider linking to media files

You can embed video and sound in a webpage using the embed tag and object tag. But these tags' use is not standardised; different browsers handle the multimedia differently. You must also size the content correctly, and the browser must have the appropriate plug-in to handle the content. An easier way to include multimedia in your webpage is by linking to it. By creating a link, your browser selects the appropriate plug-in or external application to play the media. If your browser does not know how to play the content, it asks if you want to save the media or if you want to select a program that should handle the media.

1 Consider the hypothetical webpage here. Along the page's right side are thumbnails of previous events by the fictional company. Each thumbnail is a link to its associated video.

2 Upon clicking the top thumbnail, because the hyperlink has a target attribute with _blank as its value, the video opens in a new window. Safari loads the Quicktime plug-in automatically and begins playing the video.

3 Upon clicking the link to the sample DJ music set, the MP3 file opens in a new window, and Quicktime automatically begins playing the song.

ALERT: Storing and delivering multimedia can be expensive. Videos are large, requiring ample disk space and bandwidth for your users to download the video. Either you host your own web server or, more likely, you pay someone to host your site. How much you pay depends upon your site's storage and bandwidth requirements. Including video content requires ample storage space and bandwidth. Have you ever seen the message 'bandwidth limit exceeded'? This is because someone has used too much bandwidth and must increase his or her service level. Increasing a service level costs money.

HOT TIP: In the hyperlink to the multimedia, include a target attribute with a _blank as its value. A target with this value causes the hyperlink to open in a new tab or window.

Avoid using animated GIFS

Animated GIFS, except in rare circumstances, look like hell. Do not use them.

1 Navigate to Google and search for 'animated gif' and then navigate to some of the sites. Most, if not all, of the animations will probably look amateurish and would not be a good addition to your website.

2 Look at the images below. They look terrible, but sites with animated GIFS similar to these are all too common.

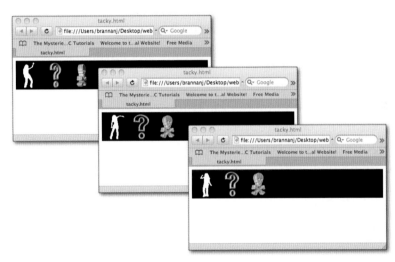

3 Now search for 'dancing baby' and try to find the dancing baby animation. Do you remember the dancing baby fad from the 1990s? The dancing baby was a demo file shipped with 3DStudio Max. This was the beginning of the 3D animation revolution, and this animated GIF found its way onto many websites which had nothing to do with babies, much less dancing babies.

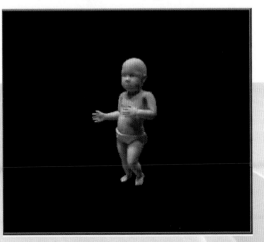

Use Flash sparingly

Avoid excessive Flash animation. Just because an animation is Flash, and not an animated GIF, does not mean the animation is somehow better than an animated GIF. You should also avoid using Flash to create your website; use HTML and CSS.

1 Refer to the Flash template shown here: interesting, but not usable. To get the full effect, you must view it in a web browser. However, just by looking at it, you should realise this template, albeit cool, is unusable.

2 The next one, also graphically dazzling, does not label any links, and requires you to click on animated circles that constantly move, making navigation extremely difficult.

3 Both these templates are brilliant Flash design, and I definitely could not do better; but they are not usable.

4 If you are an artist, a photographer for instance, then highlighting your art using a Flash template might be appropriate. For instance, consider the Flash template in the final pair. This shows a Flash template for a hypothetical photographer's site. It allows the photographer to display his or her photographs.

5 The photography website is also usable and presents the photographer's information clearly. The site's main links are along the bottom and if a user wishes to contact the artist, he or she could quite easily.

ALERT: I am over 40. You might argue my preferences for simplicity are due to my advancing age.

HOT TIP: If you learn nothing else from this book, remember, users will go to your site to fulfil a need. You usually fulfil needs with services, not amazing graphics.

DID YOU KNOW?
A recent trend in web development is something called Rich Internet Applications (RIA). In an RIA, substantial portions of the Internet application functions in a user's browser. For instance, the application used in Chapter 5, Adobe Kuler, is a rich Internet application. To load and use the application in your browser, you must have the latest Flash plug-in installed.

DID YOU KNOW?
Before emulating an RIA such as Kuler, you should ascertain if it is necessary. Kuler is an application which happens to be delivered by the Web; Kuler is not gratuitous special effects delivered using Flash. If you are delivering an application via the Web, consider an RIA. But if you simply want to use an RIA's cool features to create impressive navigation, animation and other special effects, reconsider.

155

? **DID YOU KNOW?**

The templates all come from the site FlashVillage.com and are free for members to reuse, provided they are not redistributed.

Avoid video codecs nobody has on their computer

Video codecs encode and decode digital video. When you store video, it is encoded. When a browser downloads a video, it determines which program to display the video with. If it has no codec, your browser either asks you or, if the video is embedded, it usually displays a broken link.

1 A full video codec discussion is beyond this book's scope. But go to Wikipedia (en.wikipedia.org) and search for video codec. You will find more information than you need to know.

2 There are numerous video encoding strategies. Some of the more common codecs are MPEG-1, MPEG-2, MPEG-4, RealVideo, Quicktime and Windows Media Video. While there are numerous other codes, follow this rule: if your video plays in the three most common video players, Quicktime, Windows Media Player and the VLC Media Player, most users will not have problems viewing your video.

3 Now consider videos you watch on sites such as YouTube or MetaCafe. These sites encode videos using the Adobe Flash Video codec (.flv) and require encoding the video using Flash. These videos also require Flash installed in a user's browser.

? DID YOU KNOW?

If you own a Mac, creating a video is easy. iMovie comes free with OS X. Although using iMovie is beyond this book's scope, the screenshot should illustrate how easy it is to create a web video using iMovie. Select a format, select the target delivery and export the video.

Consider putting your videos on YouTube

An easy and free way you can add multimedia to your site is through embedding the YouTube embedded video player. It is free, and YouTube provides instructions – an easy and inexpensive way to deliver multimedia. Think about it, YouTube is incurring both the storage and the delivery costs.

1 If you have not already got one, get a YouTube account.

2 Review YouTube's instructions for uploading video and creating playlists. Note, YouTube makes it easy to embed the video on an external website.

3 Embed the content on your site by adding the provided HTML snippet to your webpage's HTML.

ALERT: Embedding your video playlist using a YouTube player is potentially copyright infringement. For instance, if you embed an artist's copyrighted music video on your site, who's culpable for the copyright infringement? YouTube argues you are, as it claims it merely stores the content; users are the copyright violators according to YouTube.

Consider podcasting to deliver your multimedia

Have you ever wanted to do your own radio or television show? You can by podcasting. Podcasting, a term coined by combining iPod and broadcasting, is a common way to deliver video and audio over the Internet. The way it works is you create a video or audio show, and save it using a common audio or video format. You also create an XML file to describe the show, and then upload both to a web server.

1 Record the podcast to digital format such as MP3 or MP4.

2 Create an RSS feed which describes your podcast.

3 Create a link on your website so users can listen to your podcast. This link points to the podcast. Create another link to the RSS feed so users can subscribe to your podcast.

4 Next time you record a new podcast you replace the RSS feed. Subscribed users are automatically notified of the change and can download the new episode.

| MAY 13 | **Announcing our podcast** Subscribe to our podcast of all our productions. subscribe \| latest episode | **4** |

? DID YOU KNOW?

A user can download individual podcasts on a one-time basis or subscribe to your podcast. If a user subscribes to your podcast, then he or she is notified every time you create a new one. The user can then download the podcast at leisure. Podcasting is a good way to present more content online, and it is as inexpensive and accessible as creating a website.

? DID YOU KNOW?

An RSS feed is a text file with a .rss extension. The file contains text which describes your podcast using a language called Extensible Markup Language (XML). When you subscribe to a podcast, you subscribe to the RSS feed. Whenever the site updates the podcast you are notified and can download and play the podcast.

10 Testing your website

Introduction

After planning and developing your site, test it. Testing is as important as design and development. Testing ensures that what you designed and developed actually works. And testing should be thorough; you can consider your site tested only after you have made sure your site functions correctly, is usable and offers the functionality you envisioned it having.

Click every button, every link at least once

Test every page, even if it is a simple static HTML page where seemingly nothing can go wrong. Just because it displays when loaded in your browser does not mean it was adequately tested.

1 Consider the example page shown here. When rolling over the links on the top menu, every link is red except for the last one, Contact Me. This link is not a link at all. Had you not tested, this problem would have remained undetected.

2 Now consider what happens when a path to an image is incorrect: the images do not display. But because they have no alt tag the browser provides no alternative text describing the images. Moreover, the image dimensions are unknown and so the proper space is not preserved. Not having alt tags and not specifying an image's dimensions is sloppy.

3 Notice the final pair of pages. When you click the page's hyperlink you obtain an error. When testing, you should click every link and every button.

4 Resize the browser and review the page's appearance. Change your computer's resolution. Dream of different ways you can test your page. Just be certain to test your pages thoroughly.

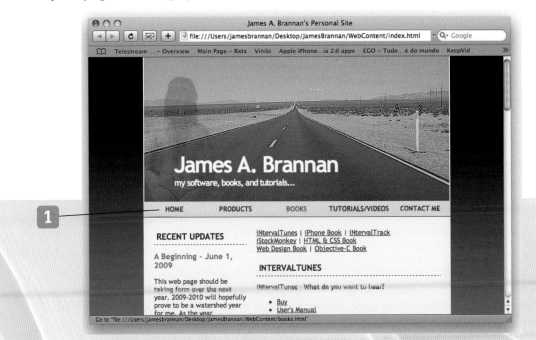

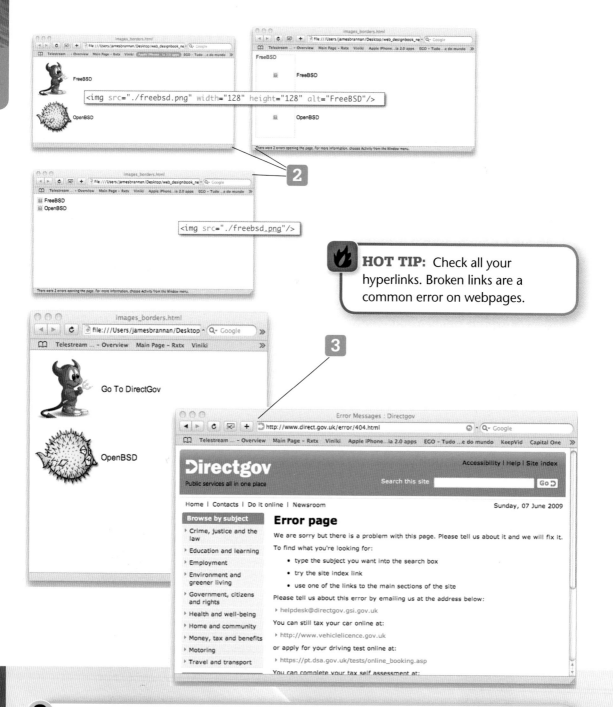

2

3

HOT TIP: Check all your hyperlinks. Broken links are a common error on webpages.

? DID YOU KNOW?

In a larger development project, testing is formalised. In smaller projects, and even some larger projects, testing webpages is an afterthought. But even if you work on a larger project, with a formal testing team, remember, they are testers not debuggers. Their job is testing your work against requirements not debugging it so it simply functions normally.

Test using more than one browser

There are arguably two, possibly three, browsers you should always test your pages in: FireFox, Internet Explorer and Safari. Depending upon your target audience, and your resources, you might also test in older browser versions. Things that function in the latest browsers might not render correctly in older browsers.

1 Consider the hypothetical page shown here. The page contains an image link. An image link is an image used as a hyperlink. The page displays nicely in Safari.

2 Now consider the next hypothetical page. Notice that FireFox adds a border around the image link.

3 Explorer also adds a border around the image link. What looked good in Safari looked poor in FireFox and Internet Explorer. Internet Explorer and FireFox add borders to the image, distinguishing the image as a hyperlink. Safari does not add a border. If you only tested on Safari, you would deploy a page with ugly blue hyperlink borders around your image.

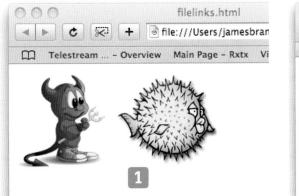

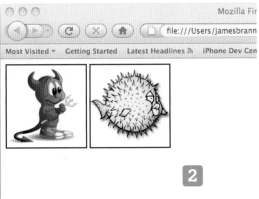

? **DID YOU KNOW?**

The problem in the example page is that the img hyperlink doesn't specifically specify that the hyperlink has no border. Safari does not render the border, Explorer and FireFox do. Fixing this error requires specifying the hyperlink has no border using CSS.

! **ALERT:** When you make mistakes in your HTML and CSS, the browser guesses how to render the page. Different browsers often guess differently, rendering your page differently. Remember, always test in different browsers.

Test your site's usability

Always test that users can use your site. If you have a large budget, you can hire users to test your site. If the site is a personal site, get friends and family or colleagues to test. Ensure the testers were not involved in the site's development though, so you can get unbiased tests.

1 Refer to the Flash template shown here. The template is downloaded from FlashVillage.com and is freely reusable if you register with the site.

2 Consider its usability. Consider the links, for instance, how would a user know which link points to the 'client history' information?

3 After blindly clicking, you eventually find the link. You could make the site more usable by labelling the hyperlinks, even if they do detract from the site's ambiance. At least provide a mouse-over tooltip that identifies the link's target when a user moves his or her cursor over the eye.

HOT TIP: Do not have testers clicking blindly. Get testers to perform scripted tasks. Can the user perform the task quickly and easily? If not, consider changing your site. A hard to use task is usually an unused task.

? DID YOU KNOW?
While I have criticised the template's usability, you have to admit, the Flash template is brilliant – even if it is not usable, in my opinion.

4 Navigate to the 'client history' page. Now consider how to return to the main menu. There are no apparent links. Intuition tells me to click on the eye again; however, you should not force users into relying upon intuition. Clearly label your links.

5 Look again at the home page. Who is the website for? What is the website about? Nothing on the home page answers these questions except for the small copyright statement at the page's lower right.

? DID YOU KNOW?
Large organisations often perform user testing early in a website's planning stages. This early usability testing helps the company design and then develop a usable site.

🔥 HOT TIP: If you wait until your site is complete, usability testing might provide you with a nasty surprise. Your site might be unusable, and a fully developed site is much harder to modify than a prototype site. You might consider usability testing when you have a prototype navigation template rather than waiting until completely developing the site. Test early and test often.

Test your site meets its requirements

Ensuring your site functions and is usable is only part of testing. As important is that your site performs the functions it was intended to perform.

1 Refer to the Bodybuilding webpage in Chapter 1 (page 28). Use cases are a good starting point if you have no formal requirements. If you have formal requirements, start with the requirements document.

2 Refer to the diagrams in Chapter 2 (pages 36 and 37). The first is an outline of the site built in later sections of Chapter 2. The second is the site map. Both diagrams provide good documents to check against the built site that follows on pages 55–65.

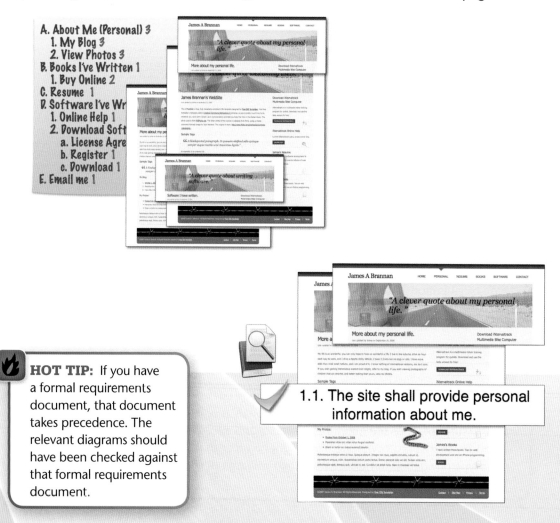

1.1. The site shall provide personal information about me.

HOT TIP: If you have a formal requirements document, that document takes precedence. The relevant diagrams should have been checked against that formal requirements document.

Validate your site's pages using the W3C's HTML Validator

Historically, HTML was not standardised. Different browsers added different features in an endless quest for web dominance. Netscape would add something brilliant, and the next Internet Explorer version would equal Netscape's brilliant feature, but add something even more brilliant. For several years, it was a browser arms race. The computer industry formed the W3C to standardise HTML, and browsers have been gravitating towards meeting the W3C's stricter standards. You should do the same. You can test that your website's HTML syntax is correct using the W3C's HTML validation service.

1 Navigate to the freecsstemplates.org website and find a template with a 'Valid XHTML' link towards the template's bottom. I am using the template entitled Gumamela.

2 Clicking the 'Valid XHTML' link opens the W3C's HTML Validator and submits the template to the application, which validates the template's XHTML.

3 If you download the template, you can choose the Validate by File Upload option to validate the page.

4 Now suppose you invalidate a couple of tags. When you validate the document, the service displays errors. Note that if you tick the 'Clean up Markup with HTML Tidy' tick box, a text area towards the page's bottom displays the corrected XHTML.

Validate your CSS style sheets using the W3C's CSS Validator

A large site's CSS templates might get large and become difficult to test. Moreover, CSS templates can include other CSS templates. Physically checking every CSS line becomes increasingly difficult as a site's size increases. The W3C's CSS Validation service automates testing your site's CSS.

1 Download a template from freecsstemplates.org. I use Gumamela again for this example.

2 Navigate to the W3C's CSS Validator at jigsaw.w3.org/css-validator.

3 Upload the template's CSS file to the service (the file with the .css extension) and click submit. The page should validate unless there is an error.

4 Introduce one or more errors to the CSS file and save it. Upload again and retest. The Validator should find your introduced errors.

W3C CSS Validation Service
W3C CSS Validator results for file://localhost/default.css (CSS level 2.1)

Jump to: Warnings (4)   Validated CSS

W3C CSS Validator results for file://localhost/default.css (CSS level 2.1)

Congratulations! No Error Found.

This document validates as CSS level 2.1 !

To show your readers that you've taken the care to create an interoperable Web page, you may display this icon on any page that validates.
Here is the XHTML you could use to add this icon to your Web page:

3

```
<p>
    <a href="http://jigsaw.w3.org/css-validator/check/referer">
        <img style="border:0;width:88px;height:31px"
            src="http://jigsaw.w3.org/css-validator/images/vcss'
            alt="Valid CSS!" />
    </a>
</p>
```

```
<p>
    <a href="http://jigsaw.w3.org/css-validator/check/referer">
        <img style="border:0;width:88px;height:31px"
            src="http://jigsaw.w3.org/css-validator/images/vcss-blue"
            alt="Valid CSS!" />
    </a>
</p>
```

(close the img tag with > instead of /> if using HTML <= 4.01)

The W3C validators are hosted on server technology donated by HP, and supported by community donations.
Donate and help us build better tools for a better web.

If you like, you can download a copy of this image to keep in your local web directory, and change the XHTML fragment above to reference your local image rather than the one on this server.

Warnings (4)

URI : file://localhost/default.css

60	Same colors for color and background-color in two contexts #menu .active a and #header h1 a
60	Same colors for color and background-color in two contexts #menu a:hover and #header h1 a
144	Same colors for color and background-color in two contexts #menu a:hover and #colTwo a:hover
144	Same colors for color and background-color in two contexts #menu .active a and #colTwo a:hover

Valid CSS information

```
body {
    margin : 0;
    padding : 0;
    background : #a0a0a3;
    font : normal small "Trebuchet MS", Arial, Helvetica, sans-serif;
    color : #9a9a9a;
}

h1, h2, h3 {
    margin : 0;
    padding : 0;
    text-transform : lowercase;
    font-weight : normal;
    color : #6c7f00;
}

h2 {
    letter-spacing : -2px;
    font-size : 1.8em;
}

p, blockquote, ol, ul {
    line-height : 180%;
    font-size : 0.9em;
}
```

4

W3C CSS Validation Service
W3C CSS Validator results for file://localhost/defaulterr.css (CSS level 2.1)

Jump to: Errors (2)   Warnings (4)   Validated CSS

W3C CSS Validator results for file://localhost/defaulterr.css (CSS level 2.1)

Sorry! We found the following errors (2)

URI : file://localhost/defaulterr.css

| 16 | h1, h2, h3 | Property marginx doesn't exist : 0 |
| 18 | h1, h2, h3 | Property text-transformzz doesn't exist : lowercase |

The W3C validators are hosted on server technology donated by HP, and supported by community donations.
Donate and help us build better tools for a better web.

Warnings (4)

URI : file://localhost/defaulterr.css

60	Same colors for color and background-color in two contexts #menu a:hover and #header h1 a
60	Same colors for color and background-color in two contexts #menu .active a and #header h1 a
144	Same colors for color and background-color in two contexts #menu .active a and #colTwo a:hover
144	Same colors for color and background-color in two contexts #menu a:hover and #colTwo a:hover

Valid CSS information

```
body {
    margin : 0;
    padding : 0;
    background : #a0a0a3;
    font : normal small "Trebuchet MS", Arial, Helvetica, sans-serif;
    color : #9a9a9a;
}

h1, h2, h3 {
    padding : 0;
    font-weight : normal;
    color : #6c7f00;
}

h2 {
    letter-spacing : -2px;
    font-size : 1.8em;
}

p, blockquote, ol, ul {
    line-height : 180%;
    font-size : 0.9em;
}
```

Remember, you cannot please everyone

You cannot please everyone. When you use the Web's latest features, ensure your webpage still functions for users with older browsers. Ensure your page is legible in all browsers, even old ones. A page does not have to be pretty, merely legible. The Web is an indispensable information source; do not exclude a group based upon disability. It is fitting this book ends with this best practice. Recall Chapter 1's mantra: provide the user with a service. You cannot create a popular service if your service only caters to a fraction of your audience. Create a website that gracefully degrades, so everyone can use your service.

1 Consider the Gumamela template at 800x600 resolution. Although not as nice as 1024x768, the page degrades and is still usable.

2 Now consider what happens when the CSS template is not applied to the page's HTML. The page, although ugly, remains legible.

Top 10 Web Design Problems Solved

Problem 1: I still don't know how to actually create a webpage. What do I do next?

You need to learn Hypertext Markup Language (HTML) and Cascading Style Sheets (CSS).

This book's purpose was teaching you how to design a website and webpage. But you cannot create the webpages you designed unless you have a basic understanding of HTML and CSS. HTML is the basic formatting language of webpages. CSS is the language for formatting an HTML created webpage's appearance; it formats a webpage's presentation. Understanding both is fundamental if you want to create webpages.

1 Open www.w3schools.com in your web browser. Now bookmark this site; it should become one of your most visited sites, as it is the most comprehensive resource on the Internet.

2 Notice it has tutorials and references on virtually every web-related technology including HTML, XHTML, CSS, XML, XML DOM, and JavaScript. This site has been my number one resource over the years and I trust it will become yours too.

3 Now, if you haven't already, buy a book on HTML and CSS. Of course I recommend *Brilliant HTML & CSS* by, ahem, James A. Brannan (published by Pearson Education, 2009) .

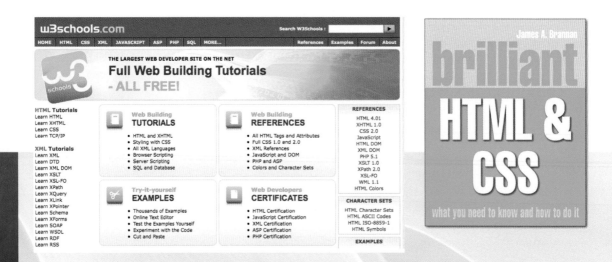

Problem 2: What do I use in HTML and CSS to create a webpage?

Although you can use programs like Word, Pages, TextPad, and TextEdit to write HTML and CSS, you will be more productive if you learn an HTML and CSS authoring tool.

The industry standard for HTML and CSS authoring is Adobe's Dreamweaver. But this application is prohibitively expensive. Luckily there are many open source alternatives, albeit none as good as Dreamweaver. What you want is a WYSIWYG that also allows editing the source.

1 Navigate to www.kompozer.net and download KompoZer. This open source web authoring software is easy to use and relatively stable.

2 Notice that you can edit a page both graphically and by modifying the source.

3 You can also edit CSS pages.

WHAT DOES THIS MEAN?

What You See Is What You Get (WYSIWYGI): A webpage editing application where you can build a page much like you would use a program like Word or Pages. Behind the scenes, the software generates the HTML needed to represent the page you lay out visually.

Problem 3: How do I edit images so they look good on a webpage?

You need to learn an image-authoring tool like Adobe Photoshop Elements or GIMP. My suggestion is Adobe Photoshop Elements, as it is inexpensive, intuitive and is recommended by lots of people. Also, buy a good book that teaches you how to use the tool you select.

1 Navigate to Adobe's website and you can download a trial copy of Adobe Elements.

2 Go to Amazon.com and search for Adobe Photoshop Elements. There are many books, including *Brilliant Adobe Photoshop Elements* by Steve Johnson (published by Pearson Education, 2009).

3 If you cannot afford Adobe Photoshop Elements, then navigate to www.gimp.org and download the GNU Image Manipulation Program (GIMP).

? DID YOU KNOW?

GIMP is an open source graphics program with a long history. It is a stable, high-quality program, albeit not as easy to use as Adobe Photoshop Elements.

HOT TIP: Before you get too creative, realise your constraints. Editing images is time consuming.

Problem 4: Where can I learn more about use case analysis?

There are hard references on use case analysis, and there are easy references. I recommend an easy reference, as use case analysis should not be difficult. Remember, because use cases focus on how users will use your site, it helps you make your website a service.

1 Refer back to Chapter 1. In this chapter I discuss requirements and use case analysis. This step is crucial to designing a website that meets users' needs.

2 Go to Google and search for 'use case analysis' and you will see many online references. Navigate to Wikipedia and you will find ample references.

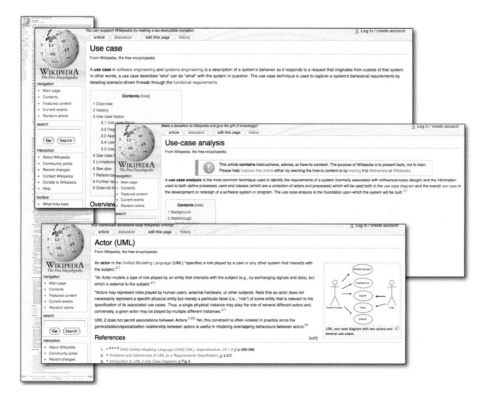

HOT TIP: Use case analysis is also used to develop rather complex systems. If you find a web reference using a complex system, keep searching – you will find a reference more applicable to web design.

3 Now, navigate to the Directgov's website (www.direct.gov.uk), by no means a fancy site, but a useful one.

4 Now notice the open source Flash Site template from FlashVillage.com. It is brilliant, but not very usable.

5 Now surmise which site probably conducted requirements and use case analysis. Requirements and use case analysis are important if you want to design a usable site that meets users' needs.

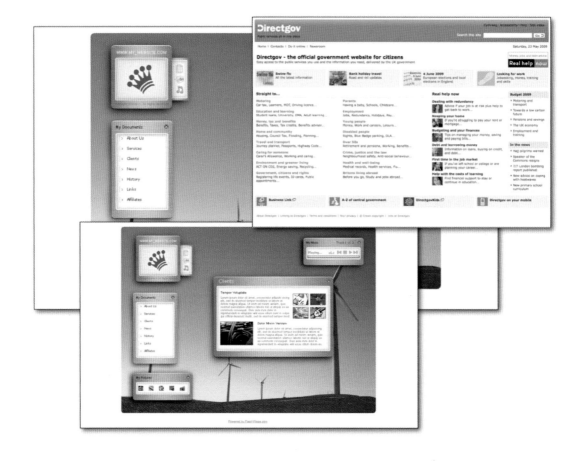

Problem 5: How do I check my work once I'm finished?

Validate your HTML and CSS using the W3C's tools. Also use your WSYIWYG's validation features.

1 Refer to Chapter 10 and review the many sites.

2 Navigate to the W3C's site and find the CSS Validation Service. You can validate your CSS style sheet using this service.

3 You can also validate your HTML page on this site.

4 Tools such as KompoZer and DreamWeaver also help validate your HTML and CSS as you write it.

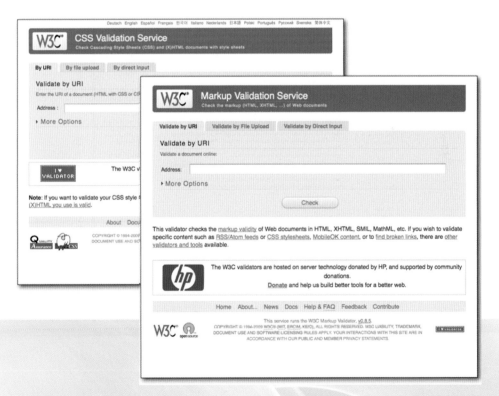

Problem 6: Nobody is visiting my site. How do I get users?

The first thing you must do is analyse who you want to be your site's users. Then analyse your site. Are you providing a service to these users?

1 Review Chapters 1 and 2; both contain information on how to design a website that meets users' needs.

2 Navigate to Wikipedia and find the 'Search engine optimization' term. There are many things you can do to make your website appear in search engines.

Problem 7: My site looks unprofessional. How do I make it appear more professional?

Consistency, accuracy, and constraint; these three terms describe a website's most important features. Throughout this book I have stressed these three features. For more information you should refer back through this book.

1. Remember, your page should appear consistent. Review Chapter 2's discussion about creating headers, footers and navigation templates.

2. Remember, your pages should be accurate. Spelling and grammatical errors make your site appear unprofessional. Broken links and other page errors also make for an unprofessional website.

3. Finally, and perhaps most importantly, remember to practise restraint. Use a consistent, appealing colour palette of no more than four or five colours. Do not use images indiscriminately and do not place them haphazardly on a webpage. Instead, use a grid and when in doubt, leave it out.

Problem 8: My website takes a long time to load. How do I fix this?

Some users might simply have bad Internet connections. But if your site loads slowly for many users, chances are there are one or more problems that cause your site's pages to load slowly. You must determine the root causes for this behaviour. All of these steps are discussed in more detail throughout this book.

1 The most likely culprits are images and other multimedia. Remember, you should optimise an image for display on the Web. If you own a tool such as Adobe Photoshop Elements, chances are it has a feature that performs these optimisations for you.

2 Consider using thumbnails that link to the original image if your site contains many images.

3 If your site includes audio and video, ensure your pages link to this multimedia rather than embed it.

4 Does your site contain excessive eye candy? Remove as many unnecessary images as possible.

5 Ensure your HTML and CSS are valid. Sometimes invalid HTML and CSS can cause a browser to load the page more slowly.

6 Ensure you picked a reliable, fast service provider. Often you get what you pay for; an inexpensive service provider might have a slow connection to the Internet and substandard server hardware.

7 If your pages contain excessive advertisements, these ads are most likely slowing your pages. Ads are usually served from a different server to yours, so fetching the ads and placing them in your page takes time.

Problem 9: I'm not very artistic, but can't afford to pay a web designer. What do I do?

First, if you haven't already, buy and read this book. Creating a professional, artistic website does not require a professional design team. Review this book's discussions on the many design tools available to you.

1. The easiest way to get started is by using a prebuilt HTML and CSS template. You can buy one or use one of the many free ones available on the Web. The website www.freecsstemplates.org is a particularly good source for free templates.

2. Instead of trying to pick your own colour scheme, let a tool like Adobe Kuler pick your palette for you.

3. Select professional looking icons from sites like www.kdelook.org and avoid cheap clipart and animated GIFS.

4. Finally, remember, eye candy is not what draws users to your site. Services attract users.

5. And don't forget Craigslist! Contrary to media hype, you can find professional help reasonably priced on Craigslist. Just be certain to protect yourself and have a fair payment worked out, like half up front and half upon delivery.

6. Finally, remember that professional looking graphics are hard and take time. The numerous Photoshop tutorials on the Web make it look easy, but trust me, it is not.

---

london craigslist > computer gigs   email this posting to a friend

WEB DESIGN

please flag with care:

Reply to: gigs-ucvdg-1251741368@craigslist.org [Errors when replying to ads?]
Date: 2009-07-05, 9:02AM BST

miscategorized

prohibited

spam/overpost

I am looking for someone to quote me a price for some sites

best of craigslist

1) Dating site (simple) which can be upgraded later
2) Local classifieds site
3) A simple membership site (theme to be confirmed)

my budget is low

- It's NOT ok to contact this poster with services or other commercial interests
- Compensation: £

PostingID: 1251741368

Copyright © 2009 craigslist, inc.   terms of use   privacy policy   feedback forum

Problem 10: How do I start?

1. Do not let this book's detail intimidate you.

2. The easiest way to begin is by simply getting started. Read the tutorials on the W3School's website. Create simple HTML and CSS pages. While important, do not use Chapter 1's emphasis on planning as an excuse not to begin designing your webpage.

3. For goodness sake, use a template! I'm this book's author, and I used a template for my site and a template for my blog. There is no shame in starting with templates.

4. The sooner you get started, the more likely it is that you will begin, and finish, your website.

5. Finally, remember this adage from bicycle racing: 'Last of the fast, best of the rest'. This describes the vast majority of cyclists on the road, the author included. We are slower than the fast cyclists, yet better than most cyclists on the road. But the thing is, by simply trying, you are in a much better position than most. I live by this adage.

6. Find a free template and just get started. Incidentally, if you use 'under construction' pages you have my forgiveness. In my humble opinion (IMHO) it is much better to get started than waiting, even if it means you use 'under construction' pages... but my official stance is still that 'under construction' pages are bad form. No matter what you do, it can't be much worse than my site (www.jamesabrannan.com), which is functional, but will not win any design awards.

USE YOUR COMPUTER WITH CONFIDENCE

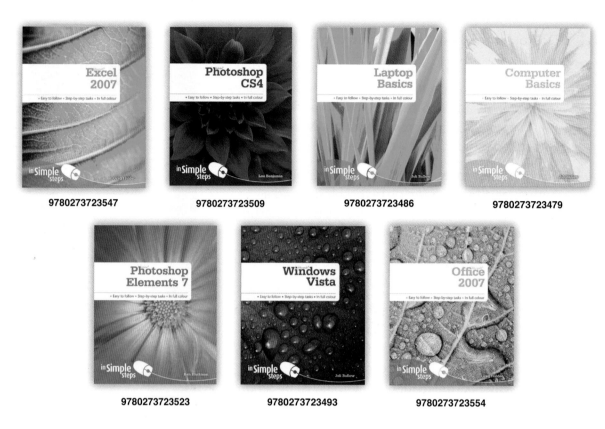

9780273723547

9780273723509

9780273723486

9780273723479

9780273723523

9780273723493

9780273723554

In Simple Steps guides guarantee immediate results. They teach you exactly what you want and need to know on any application; from the most essential tasks to master through to solving the most common problems you'll encounter.

- **Practical** – explains and provides practical solutions to the most commonly encountered problems

- **Easy to understand** – jargon and technical terms explained in simple English

- **Visual** – full colour large screen shots

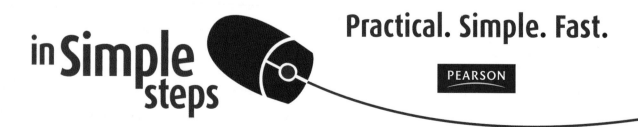